GW01424143

2000

CATCH THE
MILLENNIUM
BUG
WITH ERIC AND

YOUNG WRITERS

ESSEX

Edited by Dave Thomas

First published in Great Britain in 1999 by
YOUNG WRITERS
Remus House,
Coltsfoot Drive,
Woodston,
Peterborough, PE2 9JX
Telephone (01733) 890066

HB ISBN 0 75431 674 2
SB ISBN 0 75431 675 0

FOREWORD

Young Writers have produced poetry books in conjunction with schools for over eight years; providing a platform for talented young people to shine. This year, the Celebration 2000 collection of regional anthologies were developed with the millennium in mind.

With the nation taking stock of how far we have come, and reflecting on what we want to achieve in the future, our anthologies give a vivid insight into the thoughts and experiences of the younger generation.

We were once again impressed with the quality and attention to detail of every entry received and hope you will enjoy the poems we have decided to feature in *Celebration 2000 Essex* for many years to come.

CONTENTS

Baddow Hall Junior School

Adam Smith	36
Lewis Doe	37
Andrew Laurie	37
Emma Chatt	38
Hannah Herlihy	39
Timothy Allen	40
Bethan Anderson	41
Luke Worley	42
Jack Eagle	42
James Collins	43
Liam Messin	43
Courtney Warner-Denny	43
Stephanie Rose McPherson	44
Carlys Bedford	44
Oscar Woolnough	44
Michael Austin	45
Alice Delf	45
Holly Ringsell	46
Jared Johnston	46
Rebecca John	47
Laura Williams	47
Reece Bude	48
Daniel Entwistle	48
Nicola Burton	49
Harley Brooks	49
Sarah Daniels	50
Lucy Summers	50
Thomas Conlon	51
Christopher Hurcum	51
Martin Bagshaw	51
Joe Bellman	52
Michael Burton	52
Lee Stopher	53
Joshua Bolton	53
Freddie Chatt	54
Katy Matthewson	54

Barling Magna CP School

Caroline Evennett	54
Tom Cuthell	55
Tasha Riley	55
Alexander Dowsett	56
Ben Crofts	56
Emily Sleigh-Johnson	57
Billy Jackson	57
Thomas Brambill	58
Gemma Batty	58
Steven Sterry	58
Gemma Child	59
Chris Humphrey	59
Leanne Jones	60
Sophie Holland	60
Joe Storrar	60

Barnes Farm Junior School

Samantha Perry	61
Emma Simmonds	61
Emily Hipgrave	62

Beehive Preparatory School

Chirag Desai	62
Vivek Gupta	63
Lauren Emma Shepherd	64
Surat Dhillon	64
Lucas Came	65
Erika Padua	66
Annabel Singh	67
Hollie Cartwright	68

Boreham Primary School

Samantha Rush	68
Timothy Reyland	69
Sophie Wrigglesworth	69
Matthew Watson	70
Rebecca Martin	70

Deborah Aitken	71
Anthony Nunez	72
Thomas Nunez	72
Amy Westney	73
Katy Reyland	74
Rachel Andrew	75
Zoe Copson	76
Amelia Burns	77
Fuschia Burgess	77
Sarah Clements	78
Siân Rice	78
Christopher Hills	79
Hannah Mace	80

Earls Hall Junior School

Sarah Robinson	80
Clare Campbell	81
Jack Lidster- Woolf	81
Sarah Edwards	82
Gregory Moulton	82
Miriam Nicholas	83
Gary Derbridge	83
Kerry-Ann Jervis & Rachel Mundy	84
Holly Dixon	84
Daryl Bush	85
Russell Taylor	85
Chelsie Lewis	86
Ben Allen	86
Amanda Coban	87
Emma Howell	88
Frances Morris	88
Claire Walsh	89
Mark Howell	90
Sophie Costello & Theresa Jackson	90
Daniel Humphrey	91
Sandy Wilson	91
Charlotte Gray	92
Abigail Mitchell	92

Frinton-On-Sea Primary School

David Smith	112
Liam Battersby	112
Ross George Lilley	113
Kerry Skinner	114
Edward Evans	114
Cassie Thompson	115
Sophie Gooch	116
Thomas Brand	116
Sadie Newell	117
Leanne Gosford	117
Matthew Lindsay	118
Anthony Larvin	118
Sarah Hall	119
Andrew Webster	119

Harlowbury CP School

Abigail Alger	120
Emma Steven	120
Kylie Anne Doe	121

Milwards CP School

Martin Goodchild	121
Lee Hattersley	122
Mark Franklin	122
Melanie Dahm	123
Jonathan Stewart	123
Lauren Roberts & Ellie Bromage	124
Gemma Watson	124
Danny Milson	125
Hayley Newman	125
Paul Taylor	126
Charlotte Fargeot	126
Anna Calderon	127
Lee Tanner	127
Sarah Packer	128
Elliott Foster	128
Natasha Freeman	129

The Poems

SCIENTISTS

S cientiests, scientists, what could they be?
C alculating the numbers.
I nventing cool machines.
E ven shrinking human beings.
N ever doing as they're told.
T hey're just doing what they want to.
I sn't it cool!
S cientists are they good or bad?
T ry to be a scientist.
S cientists *emm,* shall we try it?

Matthew Bilbey (9)
All Saints CE Primary School

PIGS

Pigs can be fat
pigs can be thin
They can be black, pink
and brown also.
Pigs can live on a farm
they like people.
People like them.
Pigs can be fat,
pigs can be thin.
They can be black, pink
and brown also.

Victoria Reynolds (8)
All Saints CE Primary School

DINOSAURS

Dinosaurs, dinosaurs
in the lost world.
Nobody will see a dinosaur alive
on this planet again.
So we search for fossils
all around and
underground in
rivers and on land.

Matthew Davies (8)
All Saints CE Primary School

SPARROW

Swooping, swooping
In the air
I'm so pretty
I'm so fair.

What am I?
I'm a sparrow!

Alice Morris (7)
All Saints CE Primary School

CARS

Crashing, bashing everywhere
Cars never sleep anywhere
We always see them everywhere
And everything you do
You see a car.

Daniel Pang (7)
All Saints CE Primary School

ON HOLIDAY

I went on holiday to the sea,
A great big crab looked at me.
It bit my toe and made it bleed,
So a doctor now is what I need.

The doctor gave me a pill,
to get better, I hope that it will.
I took the toe to my mum,
and she said, 'Oh dear what have you done?'

'A crab bit my toe,' I said to her,
'but the doctor has made it better.
So now I would like my tea
if that's OK with you Mum.

And now I would like to finish my holiday.'

Catherine MacMorland (7)
All Saints CE Primary School

ANIMALS

Badgers in gardens
Badgers at night
Badgers are sensible
Badgers feed every night
Badgers eat out of your hand
and badgers dig holes to live in every night.

Candice Butcher (7)
All Saints CE Primary School

LITTLE CHILDREN

Three little children riding in a boat.
One shouted boo
and then there were two.

Two little children
standing in a line.
One ate a bun
and then there was one.

One little child
spinning round and round.
The child weighed a ton
and then there were none.

Brooke Aylen (9)
All Saints CE Primary School

TRAINS

Trains, trains, excellent trains
puffing here, puffing there
excellent trains everywhere.
Stopping here, stopping there
coupled up everywhere.
Puffing back, puffing forward
pulling coaches, pulling trucks.
Crashing here crashing there
trains crashing everywhere.
Full speed ahead.
Stop!

Kyle Townsend (9)
All Saints CE Primary School

GERBILS

Gerbils jump
Gerbils hide
And they see the high tide.

Gerbils sleep
Gerbils mate
And their babies come late.

Gerbils escape
Gerbils run.

Paul Johnson (9)
All Saints CE Primary School

BABIES

Babies here, babies there.
Babies will be everywhere.
Their mums and dads don't care when they cry.
In the shops they toddle around.

Stacey Garrett (8)
All Saints CE Primary School

TRAINS

Trains, trains everywhere,
through the station like a rocket.
Through the county and the towns,
faster than a flash of lightning.

Jack Hutchinson (8)
All Saints CE Primary School

My Dancing Class

Mrs Tipper Bullen is ready
Change your shoes!

Click, clack on the floor
tap your feet!
Shuffle your feet
forward and back.
Jump!

Change your shoes!
Heels together,
point your toes!
Slide your feet along
the floor quietly!

Change your shoes!
Hop, step,
gallop and change!
Clap your hands,
smile!

Grace Hampton (8)
All Saints CE Primary School

The Slidey Snake

Sliding here, sliding there,
Sliding almost everywhere.
It's dinnertime
Crunch, crunch,
Munch, munch.
Poor mouse.

Zachariah Noblin (8)
All Saints CE Primary School

THE OTTER

Before I was stuffed
in this silly glass cage
I could play, dance and run
chasing my brother and sister.

But now!

I can't move a leg,
my head or arm.
All I can do
is let people stare at me.

I hope my family still miss me
but I don't know
I cannot see them.
They can't see me.
I'm sorry they are left on their own
there without me.

Samantha Horrocks (8)
All Saints CE Primary School

CARS, CARS

Cars, cars everywhere,
Zooming here,
Zooming there.
Cool cars, small cars.
I don't know where they go.

Darius Dale-Davies (8)
All Saints CE Primary School

SANDY

Sandy are you lonely?
Sandy are you hot?
Sandy are you squashed?
Sandy do you think you're sweet?
Sandy are you cold or damp?
Sandy have you got brown eyes?

I wonder what she'd say.

No, I'm not lonely watching you.
No, I'm not hot in my lovely sawdust bed.
No I'm not squashed in a space like this.
I do not know if I am sweet.
I am warm and dry in this glass cage.
My eyes? I have never looked in a mirror.

Rebecca Robinson (7)
All Saints CE Primary School

THE GULL

Unable to move I stand all day.
I see boys and girls chatting.
I see children staring at me.
I see children working and playing
and I feel sad.

Unable to move I think all day.
I think about catching fish.
I think about swimming in the sea.
I think about flying in the sky
and I wish that I could see my family.

Kelly Daines (9)
All Saints CE Primary School

SANDY THE CLASSROOM GERBIL

Sandy are you bored?
Sitting in that cage doing nothing.
Sandy are you lonely?
With no one to play with at all.
Sandy are you sad?
In your cage, with only us to look at.
Sandy are you unhappy?
When we are not here
I wonder?

Maria Russell (8)
All Saints CE Primary School

SANDY

Sandy is fluffy, cream and sweet,
contented and happy.
Meets walls, crawls through them,
has a hang out,
but where is it?
She gets hot,
crawls out to have some water,
then curls up to watch the Literacy Hour.

Hannah Grant (8)
All Saints CE Primary School

TOWER HILL V MALDON SAINTS

At eight in the morning my alarm goes off,
Thinking about the grand kick-off.
I crawl out of bed as excited as could be,
At the back is it Will, or could it be me?
I wait for breakfast, it should be toast,
As I hope that this time I won't hit the post.
Aaron's in goal, no doubt about that,
Up front is Kieran, midfield is Matt.
I'm in defence with Liam and Will,
I hear the crowd cheer, 'Come on Tower Hill.'
Ollie's with the ball, he passes it back,
But he makes a mistake, Saints on the attack.
We block them down, I pass it to Aaron,
He picks it up but then comes Darren.
Darren from Saints, I should say,
Aaron rolls the ball to me but Darren's in my way.
He's taken the ball, he runs to the goal,
Kicks it past Aaron, oh dear, it's a goal.
We're 1-0 down, we take our kick off,
It's Kieran with the ball, watch him whiz off!
He runs to the keeper, taps it in,
1-1 now, but we need a win!
We get kick off in this next half,
Oh, it's our penalty! They make a path.
I will take it, the manager thinks I should,
I think I will score, I know I could.
I run up to the ball but it hits the post,
But Steve scored the rebound, that's what matters most.
Full time is now here, we're cheered by the mums,
But what we really wanted is the cup that finally comes!

Jack Gladas (8)
All Saints CE Primary School

DINOSAURS

Dinosaurs are big, dinosaurs are small.
In the Jurassic period, T-rexes were roaming.
Nobody knows for sure when dinosaurs died out.
Oh I wish I could see one.
Stegosaurus and Triceratops are my favourite.
A Triceratops charging at a tree!
Up in the sky a Pterodactyl was gliding.
Rackety plates of a Stegosaurus,
shimmering thorough the darkness of night.

Christopher Moon (8)
All Saints CE Primary School

THE GULL

I am hungry,
I am sad and lonely
just standing on this dead log
and see children playing ball
and hopscotch and that is all.
I need fish and want to play
and to see my family
but it is too sad to think about it.
All day and night.

Jade Mason (9)
All Saints CE Primary School

THE HONEY BUZZARD'S THINKING IT

I look at the honey buzzard and it's probably thinking about the life
it once had before.
I am thinking about the life I once had
soaring over the mountains.
I think it's sad.
I am sad.
I think it's bored.
I am bored.
I feel upset.
I can see tears rolling down its eyes.
Yes, I am crying.
My feathers are sticking to my face.
I can't move.

Rebecca Mallett-Vickers (9)
All Saints CE Primary School

KING ARTHUR

King Arthur brave.
King Arthur strong.
Pulling a sword from a stone.
Made him able to be on the throne.
Firstly working with a herd of cattle.
Then winning 100 battles.
When he was too old to lead
Retired and sadly died.

Matthew Wilks (8)
All Saints CE Primary School

SANDY THE CLASSROOM PET

Trapped in my cage in this noisy classroom,
as I dig in this cramped, small space,
surrounded by noise and naughtiness,
for now I am getting very old.

But now I'm getting to like it here
with my owner looking after me.
I have a pot full of food
and a lovely drink.
As I try and dream and think,
so now I can happily live my life.

Joseph Thurgood (8)
All Saints CE Primary School

THE GULL

Once I was alive,
I felt I was only five
I thought I had a never ending life.

Now I am done,
I don't have lots of fun
I feel I am the only one here.

I miss the seas,
And the light little breeze
I wish my family was right here.

Belinda Armstrong (9)
All Saints CE Primary School

SANDY THE CLASSROOM PET

When I watch I want to
be a human, then I can
jump and talk.
I wish I could work.
When I am snoring I cannot
hear a thing.
I wake up and cannot
see a thing, apart
from the sunset falling.
When the children come back
I go to sleep again.

Oliver Hylands (8)
All Saints CE Primary School

THE GULL

I am unable to move,
I stand all day.
I'm cold hungry and lonely,
I want some friends to play.
I watch the children write,
And just stare and feel sad.

John Heard (9)
All Saints CE Primary School

SANDY THE GERBIL

Sandy is very fluffy,
She makes tunnels with cardboard tubes,
She is small, hot and hungry,
Can you touch me?
No thank you
She must be bored and lonely.

Thomas Hall (8)
All Saints CE Primary School

WEASEL, WEASEL

Weasel, weasel how nice you are.
Fine fur you've got.
Big eyes you've got.
Sharp teeth you've got.
Standing on rocks watching people playing.
It's good to be a weasel.

William Root (9)
All Saints CE Primary School

THE GULL

I'm unable to move,
I stand all day,
I am always sitting watching the children.
I am always watching the teachers on playground duty.
I see children playing football
and remember I'm only a gull.

Nicole Barden (8)
All Saints CE Primary School

THE SEAGULL

I was once gliding beside the sea
but now I am stuffed.
I was once landing next to a bush
and when I landed I saw a man with a long brown tube.
I was shot.
I never saw that man again.
I was taken to a museum
then someone took me to a school.
It is very hot in here.
I've got an itch on my back and I'm thinking,
'Can someone scratch my feathers please?'
And here I am.

Joshua Lumley (8)
All Saints CE Primary School

THE HONEY BUZZARD

I can imagine the honey buzzard swooping through the trees.
Doing whatever it wants.
But now I can see it in a glass box.
Stuck.
I can see in its eyes that it wants to be back
swooping through the trees I am sure it feels sad.
I know it feels sad and upset
and it misses its family.

Alex Lewis (9)
All Saints CE Primary School

DEAD OR ALIVE

I remember the day when I played
but now I'm stuck in a glass cage.
I was jumping around.
Not now I'm dead.

I remember the time when I was sniffing in bins.
I'm not now, I'm dead.

I remember the times when I was fed.
Not now, I've been stuffed.

I remember, remember so well
playing with all my badger mates.

Emily Kate Hedgecock (7)
All Saints CE Primary School

I'M A STUFFED STOAT

I'm a stoat, I'm cute and sweet
and I've got soft fur.
I had a lovely home with my mum and dad.
I've got a small tail, it's got a brown bit on the end
and it sticks up.
I've got small teeth but big fangs.
But now it's different, all stuffed and a wire in my tail.
I'm in a hot, horrible classroom with people looking at me
and me still looking at them.

Carl Strathie (8)
All Saints CE Primary School

THE HONEY BUZZARD

I'm looking at a honey buzzard
It's staring back at me.
I look in its eyes and I can see its family.
I can see the old bird's life.
Soaring high in the blue sky,
up, up, up and up.
Until it can't fly any higher.
Goes down to kill its prey and eat it for dinner.
It chomps and it chews until dinner is over.
Then it flies into the sky again.

I'm looking at a honey buzzard
it is looking back at me.
I wish it was alive
but I'm afraid it's dead.
It's so sad looking at the dead.

Joshua Whitrod (9)
All Saints CE Primary School

THE OTTER

Once I was swimming in lakes and streams.
But now I'm in a cage, a glass cage
and in a classroom.
Children's faces staring and studying me.
Oh how much I miss those streams and lakes
and how I hate being dead.
But it's better than being in a museum.
My family is long gone.
It is very, very lonely in this glass cage.
I want to be free again as I used to be.

Matthew Holmes (7)
All Saints CE Primary School

BADGER

I am a badger under the ground.
Digging holes, down, down and down.
All my friends wake me up every morning
I always eat juicy earthworms.
But now I'm dead, I am stiff and still
and everybody stares at me
and people sketch me with chalk pastels,
sketching pencils and oil crayons.
I come from a museum stuffed with fur and wire.
After the people had me I was taken back to the museum.

Pearl Read (8)
All Saints CE Primary School

STUCK!

I don't like being in a glass case.
I feel trapped, stuck and longing to get out.
It's horrid this old fish really stinks.
I really, really hate it in this classroom.
Lots of faces staring at me
and the bumpy car journey.
Arghhh!
Here we go again!
Bump, bump, bump.

Emma Plunkett (8)
All Saints CE Primary School

A Seagull's Life

One day I was flying.
Something came out of the tree, it was a person.
The person came, he got me in a net and shot me with a black tube.
Now I am in a museum. A teacher came and took
                              me back to her school.
There were lots of children looking at me, sketching me
                              and studying me.
It was scary. Some children were touching me now.
I was very afraid. I can see all the children.
The children say goodbye to me.
I go back to the museum where I belong.

Lucy Georgina Taylor (9)
All Saints CE Primary School

Otter

Once I was going to get some fish.
A man in a bush had a gun
and there's me on the ground.
Someone found me and took me to a museum
and they stuffed me.
A school wanted to study me.
Faces all around me.
Back to the museum.

Ritchie Mark Wells (7)
All Saints CE Primary School

AN ORDINARY DAY

The playful crowds,
The noise far away,
The heat unbearable,
An ordinary day,
At school far away.

The teacher talking,
The children far away,
But the toys taken away,
An ordinary day,
In a class far away.

The teacher dismisses them,
As they trudge out of school,
At the end of a school day,
An ordinary day,
Out of the gate and far away.

Ross Bissell (11)
All Saints CE Primary School

HAMSTER

Hamster called nibbles
playing at night.
Always waking Mum,
loving having fights.
Like chewing on his cage
but not now.
Not faces looking at them.
It is faces looking at me.

Gemma Cheek (7)
All Saints CE Primary School

IT'S ALL OVER

It's all over, over for them
deep in my soul I feel sorry
and ashamed. But they are
different. They're Jews, they must
be burned. Just as I must
take orders, it's part of life.

I put on an expressionless
face and collect up the wood.
I pity them but, as commanded,
I throw the wood in, straw and all.
I feel terrible but one by one I
push them in.

I strike the match and hear
them cry, but I throw the match
in and watch their bodies burn
like paper.

As I said before it's all over,
over for them. I watch them, watch
them die. At last they're dead and
I walk away with a heavy heart.

Hannah Corby (10)
All Saints CE Primary School

NIBBLES THE HAMSTER

The hamster is chewing his cage
and he plays all day and night.
He plays all night with is friend Fred.

Jamie Baker (9)
All Saints CE Primary School

THE STOAT

I've got an itch on my back,
but I can't scratch it
as I used to
because I'm stuck stiff as a rock.
My tail aches with pain
because I have to keep it very,
very still.
My eyes have been replaced with
glass marbles
but I can still see the faces
of children.
I can feel the hands of
children stroking me
like my mother used to lick me.

Sophie Kennedy (8)
All Saints CE Primary School

LIFE AND DEATH

I once was a playful otter running on the sand.
And then I heard the click of a bullet and there I lay.
Somebody paid a lot of money to stuff me.
Now I'm in a dull classroom looking out at people studying me
and rubbing me.
I hate it there's a bit of smelly fish and I don't like it very much.
My family are long gone.

Robyn Ellison (8)
All Saints CE Primary School

THE RAINFOREST LANDSCAPE

We're all changing the landscape
  And we now do not care.
The plants, the shrubs, the wildlife
  The rainforest isn't there.

All the trees have died,
  The marks where we have been.
We've left behind our memories,
  The sights that we have seen.

Remember the tall trees,
  That towered in the sun?
We look upon the bare brown earth,
  And see what man has done.

Chlöe Mayhew (11)
All Saints CE Primary School

LIFE OR DEATH

I was once roaming around in water
But now I'm full of soft stuffing
With a million people staring at me.
I wish I was still munching a nice juicy fish skeleton
And playing and drinking in the water with all my friends!

Curtis Patching (8)
All Saints CE Primary School

LONELINESS

Being lost in an enormous place,
With no one you know,
People around you,
Who have different faces,
The ceiling is a long way up,
It's a circular building
And you're right in
The middle of everyone.
There's no one there,
You are only three years old,
You'll just stand there until
Someone comes.
But no one comes to your rescue.
'Help, help!'
You shout,
'Someone needs to come,
I am all alone.'

Helen Gardner (10)
All Saints CE Primary School

NIBBLES

Nibbles like to nibble things,
swing around and hide.
Sleeps all day and night.
Plays around and makes sounds
very soft and cuddly and hangs
from the side of his cage

Nicola Buckby (8)
All Saints CE Primary School

ALONE

Being alone is a bad experience
I've been there myself
I feel
Lonely
Isolated
Invisible
Unwanted
Deserted
It's like being a magnet but only the bad attracted
My mind is empty and all I can think of is . . .
Sadness
No parents to care for me
No friends to laugh with, just me all
Alone
It's like living in a world of fear and sadness
And
Although freedom is a long way away
Now
I know I'll get there one day.

Zoë Adams (10)
All Saints CE Primary School

SEAGULL

Once I was with my family, flying over the sea.
Now I'm in this plastic cage with faces looking over me.
It was pleasant with my family, it was cosy at home.
Now I'm upset, I have nowhere else to go.

Joanna Butcher (9)
All Saints CE Primary School

NO ONE KNOWS

Please, can you hear me?
No one's here to help.
No one cares,
I'm all alone
I'm on my own.

No one's there for me
Having to face my problems
on my own
Living with my fears
as my only friend.

Fighting for freedom,
To be with anyone,
One thing for sure
I haven't got a friend
Not one!

Emily Wiggins & Emma Lockwood (11)
All Saints CE Primary School

THE SEA

I saw the blue sea it was warm
and I saw a dolphin playing
with friends in the sea.
I saw an octopus.
I saw a sea horse and it took me back.

Donna Frost (9)
All Saints CE Primary School

THE LONELY SEAGULL

I loved to watch the roaring
sea washing the rock.
I was flying around the lonely
bedside beach and I loved water
splashing over me.
I missed my open family
why children look over me.
People loved to touch my furry
coat while I was thinking about
my family.
I missed my nest more than people.

Aaron Ostridge (8)
All Saints CE Primary School

SEAGULL

I feel free when I fly,
I feel hungry when I land on the sea,
It feels a bit dangerous,
I faint,
Soon they take me to the museum,
It feels painful when they operate on me,
Soon I am stuffed,
People are watching me,
I feel a bit frightened,
Back to the museum.

Rachel Cheung (8)
All Saints CE Primary School

A Red Nose Day Poem

R emember Red Nose Day?
E xciting day for all,
D ays like these are always fun.

N oses are red, for Red Nose Day,
O pals are red too,
S eas have patches of red in them,
E aster's here and we know that.

D ays like these, fun like I've said before,
A dding a red face, jumper and trousers,
Y esterday, we didn't have a Red Nose Day,
    (because there's only one and that's today.)

Emma Levis (10)
All Saints CE Primary School

The Millennium

Banging, shouting, laughing,
Everybody's excited with smiles on their faces,
Fireworks go off in the night.
Children singing, church bells ringing,
At midnight the lights go out,
People count from ten to one,
And then the lights go back on,
Babies screaming, toddlers dreaming,
This is the end of the day,
But there'll be plenty of this 100 years later.

Amanda Nicholson (9)
All Saints CE Primary School

The Shadow

When I lay in bed I see the
 Shadow.
When I wake up I see the
 Shadow.
When I walk down the street I see the
 Shadow.
When I play football I see the
 Shadow.
When I am playing in the park I see the
 Shadow.
When I walk up the stairs I see the
 Shadow.
When I look in the mirror I find out
 I am the shadow.

Kieran Balaam (11)
All Saints CE Primary School

Red Nose Day

R ed is for the charity for people who live in boxes,
E ver wondered what they eat? *Nothing!*
D eath is what they think is going to happen to them.

N o one can know what they're going through,
O nly you can help by giving 50p or £1,
S lowly they die each day, *you* can save their lives,
E veryone should sponsor, like me and you.

D ay and night they hunger,
A nd now it's your chance to sponsor,
Y oung and old, you can save lives!

Laura Banks (11)
All Saints CE Primary School

IT WAS EIGHTY YEARS AGO

It was eighty years ago,
Fighting,
Fighting through muddy floods in the dirty trenches.
Crying,
Crying while we painfully watched our lives go to waste.
Dying,
Dying without saying a true goodbye.
Fighting,
Then everything came to a huge halt . . .
It was eighty years ago.

Rhiannon Hughes (11)
All Saints CE Primary School

ME

I am a small voice
That nobody will listen to.
Small and unimportant.
Unwanted.
A castaway.
I am abandoned.
Lonely on my own.
No one there.

Ben Ellison (10)
All Saints CE Primary School

SEAGULL

One moment I am flying over the sea
Now I am in a glass cage.
I was free with my family
Free to go wherever I wanted,
But now I am stuck
And people are drawing pictures of me.
But the seagull they are looking at is not the real me,
The seagull that is me is someone who is happy on the sea flying
with its family
Not someone who is in a glass cage and watching people study it.

Rebecca Kent (8)
All Saints CE Primary School

TITANIC

They said Titanic was unsinkable
But that was a lie
Titanic hit an iceberg
And many were to die
Not enough boats for everyone
In them people began to cry.

Kirsty Jackson (11)
All Saints CE Primary School

Party 2000

The new Millennium is going to start
for us to celebrate.
With joy, laughter and tears,
remembering those happy years.

The 31st of December we say
12, 11, 10, 9, 8, 7, 6, 5, 4, 3, 2, 1,
Happy New Year!
Pops, bangs and fireworks
all gathered in one
            and a burst of champagne.

Ushma Kubavat (10)
All Saints CE Primary School

My Mind

In the dark, dark room of my mind,
I keep searching for the door out.
The wall is smooth like glass.
I am looking for a door but it is too dark to see.
What am I looking for?
Round and round, beating on the walls,
I have found it,
Light pouring in, I am out.
Free!

Harriet McColm (10)
All Saints CE Primary School

IS ANYBODY THERE?

People never play with me
They always leave me out
I'm really scared and lonely
They're going to beat me up
Is anybody out there?
Please come and help
There they are . . .
Whispering.
They're laughing in my face
Is anybody out there?
Does anybody care?

Frances Sarah Daniels (11)
All Saints CE Primary School

THE STREET

This is the road I walk up every day,
But today it seems different in some way.
The trees are bare, although that's not very rare.
It's wintertime. I see snow melting on the yellow lines.
The slippery, shiny ice sends a shiver down my spine.
The last leaf falls silently off the tree.
It blows around like a twister in a storm and lands by me.

Holly Lynch & Ellena Crozier (10)
All Saints CE Primary School

ALONE

I'm sitting in the coldest, darkest corner
of a room
all alone
waiting, waiting
waiting to hear the sound of footsteps
hoping, hoping
hoping to hear the sound of footsteps
wanting, wanting
wanting to hear the sound of footsteps
I slowly rise
walk to the other side
suddenly I see light
I follow it
I'm walking down a never-ending tunnel
waiting, waiting
waiting to hear the sound of voices
hoping, hoping
hoping to hear the sound of voices
wanting, wanting
wanting to hear the sound of voices
needing, needing
needing to hear the sound of voices.

Suddenly I hear the sound of footsteps and voices
but that is just my mind
because
I'm
Alone!

Kaylee Satchell (11)
All Saints CE Primary School

WHITE DIAMONDS

White diamonds splashing from great heights.
Silver-green moss. Golden grass.
Splashing from rock to rock.
Smooth stone.
Water, like white silk looks like smooth cream . . .
It's like carving lovely diamonds.

Ryan Hales (10)
All Saints CE Primary School

THE SEVEN AGES OF MAN

First I was a baby,
A loud, whiny child,
Soon a happy schoolboy,
Mad and running wild.
Next I am a teenager,
A cool, funky dude,
Now I am a student,
Always in a mood.
Now I'm buying a wedding ring,
A costly one at that,
I'm going to get a job,
I've got to buy a hat.
I am a grandfather now,
I am getting older by the day,
I'll soon be lying on my deathbed,
On the 17th of May.

Adam Smith (11)
Baddow Hall Junior School

TUTANKHAMEN

Turn around, turn around
Touch the case
Tutankhamen
Stares you in the face.

His mask so big
It's blue and gold
It's still in top shape
But it's very, very old.

His treasures all around him
It's a wondrous sight.
How did he die?
Was he buried at night?

Tutankhumen's
Been brought out of his case,
They're undoing the bandages
He's got a rotting face.

Lewis Doe (11)
Baddow Hall Junior School

A LIMERICK

There once was a man called slim,
Who was searching for food in the bin.
He was searching so fast,
He went to the past
And I wondered what happened to him.

Andrew Laurie (10)
Baddow Hall Junior School

THE TURNING OF THE SEASONS

Spring

The snow has melted.
The spring has come.
The sun is shining.
It's time for fun.

There are bouncing lambs
There are fluffy chicks.
It is getting hotter.
Wow spring's gone quick.

Summer

Summer has come.
Shells buried in the sand.
Everyone turns around.
They hear the big brass band.

Sunrises every morning.
Sunsets each night.
Stars glisten as the moon shines
But they all have their own light.

Autumn

Leaves are turning orange and red.
They fall to the ground.
As we walk through the wood
They are crunching all around.

It's getting colder
Always wrap up warm.
Quick start running
There's going to be a storm.

Winter

The roads are icing up
Snow is starting to fall.
There are lots of accidents
It's really got too cool.

Christmas is coming,
Presents to buy.
We are all in a rush
then we all breathe a sigh.

Emma Chatt (9)
Baddow Hall Junior School

GERBIL ESCAPE

The gerbil escaped one day
He ran around the house
We chased him into every room
Oh no! He's under the bed.

He rushed, he dashed and hurried.

I was worried.
I was scared.
I shivered and shook.
I heard a scuffling - it was him.

He rushed, he dashed and hurried.

I shut the door
I went to catch him.
He was caught
and put back in his cage.

He rushed, he dashed and hurried.

Hannah Herlihy (9)
Baddow Hall Junior School

MY SILLY CATS

My cats are sleeping on the grass
Still and quiet, looking up.
Get up and scratch to come in.
Steal five prawns -
Get thrown out!

Still and quiet.
Catching butterflies.
Falling in the pond.

Gazing down in the fish pond,
Said Cat One, 'Which shall I choose?'
Said Cat Two, 'I'm having that one.'

Both found
Both terrorised.

Still and quiet.
Catching butterflies.
Falling in the pond.

Looking round
Saw bird
Ran after small bird
Didn't look
Hit tree!

Still and quiet.
Catching butterflies.
Falling in the pond.

Get inside and look around
Find his bedroom
On to the window sill
Jump out open window . . .
Fall down . . . down . . . down . . .

Still and quiet.
Catching butterflies.
Falling in the pond.
Fall down . . . down . . . *hit!*
Up and dig the rose bush
Threatened
Run away . . . and away
Up his slide.

Still and quiet.
Catching butterflies.
Falling in the pond.

Slide down
Crash!
Through fence
Run away
Silly cats!

Still and quiet.
Catching butterflies.
Falling in the pond.

Timothy Allen (9)
Baddow Hall Junior School

ICE

Ice is like snow except colder.
It melts into water like ice-cream
And is no longer there.
Sometimes it's not by water at all.
It is like frost except see-through.
It is frozen water outside.

Bethan Anderson (8)
Baddow Hall Junior School

I SHOULD LIKE TO PAINT . . .

I should like to paint,
the coldness of some grass blowing in the breeze.
The smell of pizza cooking in the oven.
The taste of burgers in rolls, *yum, yum!*
The touch of the wind blowing through my hair.
The howl of a husky growling in the snow.
The feel of a furry cat rubbing against my thigh.
The creaking of a creaky door opening wide.
The excitement of some children going on holiday.
The sound of some water splashing against the shore.
The snapping of a crocodile opening and shutting his jaws.

Luke Worley (8)
Baddow Hall Junior School

FROST

As glittery as silk.
As light as feathers.
It covers all things like a white cake.
Sprinkling leaves.
Covering tree branches with velvet.
It flutters like a piece of paper in the night.
It is smooth when it lands
But . . .
It kills plants with a dinosaur touch.

Jack Eagle (7)
Baddow Hall Junior School

I SHOULD LIKE TO PAINT . . .

I should like to paint,
the taste of a fish.
The noise of a butterfly flying in the sky.
The singing of a blackbird perching on a branch.
The sound of a slithering snake.
The smell of a jaguar racing through the forest.
The flapping of a bluebird swooping through the air.

James Collins (7)
Baddow Hall Junior School

CHEETAH

Yellow fur like the sun in the morning.
With spots as black as night.
As quick as a sports car on full power.
With claws as sharp as knives.
As strong as a boxer.
Sometimes as sly as a fox.
It kills its prey like stabbing pitchforks in its neck.
With teeth as strong as metal.

Liam Messin (7)
Baddow Hall Junior School

WIND

Wind blows across the land like a rocket.
It blows away bags and knocks down trees like a steamroller.
Whistling water, rushing down a stream
Cold as an ice pop.

Courtney Warner-Denny (8)
Baddow Hall Junior School

BLACK NIGHT

The black night, is black as a black cat,
Night is black as a bin liner.
Night is black as coal.
Night is black as a chimney sweep.
Black night is as black as black paint.
It is so black!
The night is black as a bin liner, stretched over the world.
It is a big face ruling all.

Stephanie Rose McPherson (7)
Baddow Hall Junior School

SNOW

Snow is like a white blanket on the ground.
As cold as ice.
It touches you like a kiss.
Settling down like a sheet on a bed.
As deep as a mattress.
Shining like frost.

Carlys Bedford (8)
Baddow Hall Junior School

I SHOULD LIKE TO PAINT . . .

I should like to paint,
the sound of lamb cooking.
The smell of a hippo wallowing in the mud.
The taste of chocolate and cabbage, past their expiry date.
The feel of a rhino's horn.

Oscar Woolnough (7)
Baddow Hall Junior School

THE SUN

As strong as a blazes
So still as air
As yellow as a banana
The sun lay in thin air.

As heavy as an elephant
As big as Saturn, Venus and Mars
Hotter than an oven on full blast
The sun lay in thin air.

As strong as a blaze
So still as air
As yellow as a banana
The sun lay in thin air.

Michael Austin (8)
Baddow Hall Junior School

SOFTLY

Softly the mouse scuttled on her way.
Softly the sun rose for a new day.
Softly the bird sung a beautiful tune.
Softly the light shone from the moon.

Softly I slid across the sand.
Softly I held on to your hand.
Soft as the hair of a lady,
but not as soft as a newborn baby.

Alice Delf (9)
Baddow Hall Junior School

I SHOULD LIKE TO PAINT . . .

I should like to paint
the walking of the
tiny bugs.
The swirling of the
giant winds.
The moves of the
huge octopus.
The heat of the
blazing fire.
The beating of the
pumping heart.
The slyness of the
sneaky fox.

Holly Ringsell (7)
Baddow Hall Junior School

LOUDLY

Loudly the dog barked with excitement
Loudly the man shouted at his son
Loudly the bully said 'Give me your lunch!'
Loudly the car zoomed on the road

Loudly the train runs on the track
Loudly the bomb exploded
Loudly the horn honks - but loudest of all
Is an aeroplane crashing onto the school.

Jared Johnston (9)
Baddow Hall Junior School

THE YAB-NAB BIRD

Yabski-Nabski, flying through the jungle
Snakes below, canopy above.
Yab-Nab! Yab-Nab!
Eggs all spotty - legs all dotty
Beak all stripy, sabre tooth spiky
Yab-Nab! Yab-Nab!
Tail feathers bright, shining in the moonlight
Bright green tongue, having good fun.
Yab-Nab! Yab-Nab!
Claws all sharp, sharp as darts
Climbing up the lip-nip tree
Yab-Nab! Yab-Nab!
Don't look down!
Yab-Nab! Eek!

Rebecca John (10)
Baddow Hall Junior School

FROST

Frost like a gloomy passage glowing
A bunch of bushes, twiggy and bushy
Frost like gates opening as you pass
Sharp as a fireball flying through the air
Frost like a puff of smoke.

As soft as a feather when you blow it
Like stage lights glistening as you perform
Frost - a swimming bath of water sparkling.

Laura Williams (8)
Baddow Hall Junior School

THE SEVEN AGES OF MAN

At first a happy baby
Lying in my cot.

Next I'm a schoolchild
Playing football, having lots of shots.

Then I'm a teenager worrying about my looks
At school I have to carry lots of books.

Then I'm at University training to be a vet
Then I'm a vet treating sick pets.

Then I'm an old man
Building a house extension
Going down the post office
getting my pension.

Reece Bude (10)
Baddow Hall Junior School

FROST

Frost - colder than a snowflake
Like a crystal in a sparkling silver cup
As slippery as water
As smooth as the inside of a shell
As white as a clean tooth
As breakable as glass.

Daniel Entwistle (7)
Baddow Hall Junior School

THE SEVEN AGES OF MAN

First a bawling baby
Sucking on a dummy
Next a small schoolchild
Crying for its mummy
Then a swearing teenager
Smoking in the break
At last the wedding bells ring
Is this a big mistake?
Now all I need is a job
I ended up a vet
It's time for my retirement now
I haven't lost my memory yet
Next I'm at the stage, just before death
I'm all crooked and old
My legs are shrinking, my back is a hump
But at least I'm not going bald!

Nicola Burton (10)
Baddow Hall Junior School

WIND

Wind whistles like a bird
It sounds like a wolf howling
on top of a cliff
Wind is as fast as a roadrunner
Wind is as cold as the fridge
It's like a giant mouth
blowing really hard.

Harley Brooks (7)
Baddow Hall Junior School

FROST

Frost as sticky as glue
Like a leaking tap when it melts
It shimmers down to the ground
like a snowflake
Frost glittering and sparkling
like the moon.
As thin as a pencil lead
As soft as silk
Fluttering down from the sky
Brushes and taps on a sleeping child's window
Wakes her with a scream of delight
Drifting past a window.

Sarah Daniels (7)
Baddow Hall Junior School

MY ACT

Waiting not knowing what part I will be
Sitting there wondering what lines I will read.
Everyone finally knows who they'll be
Now comes the hard stuff . . . listen to me!

Learning my lines like there's no tomorrow,
Singing out loud my songs, my voice soars like a swallow
Trying on my panto clothes seeing if they will fit for this year's show.
At last the first night arrives and we are all raring to go.
The curtains open . . . here we go!

Lucy Summers (10)
Baddow Hall Junior School

In My Bedroom You Will Find

A stale jam sandwich
A chewed up pen
A microscope
A dissected fly
A half size guitar
An unmade bed
Seven pairs of socks (not in the cupboard)
And a water pistol under my pillow.

Thomas Conlon (10)
Baddow Hall Junior School

Snow

Snow, as white as a blank piece of paper
covering a whole field
Icicles like decorations hanging from
a Christmas tree
Fall like small bells twinkling
Melt like a puddle of ice-cream
Freezing once more into a swimming pool.

Christopher Hurcum (8)
Baddow Hall Junior School

The Boy Called Sam

There once was a boy called Sam
who ate all of his mum's home-made jam.
He filled up the jars with crimson toy cars
and miniature Mars chocolate bars.

Martin Bagshaw (9)
Baddow Hall Junior School

FROST

Frost as glittery as sparkly sugar in the sunlight
As soft as a mouse.
It covers like white sugar falling from the sky.
It glows with a mystical light like the moon.
Sharp as barbed wire.
Frost, cold as rock
Frost shimmers like icicles dropping
from the sky.
It has no friends because it kills.

Joe Bellman (7)
Baddow Hall Junior School

CAT

As soft as a bed
Eyes as bright as light.
Claws like spikes in a hole
A purr as quiet as the sea.
A tail like the swaying wind
Ears like mountains with snow on top.
A nose as black as night with a moon
on the side.
Whiskers like swords in a stone.
He jumps like the waves on the sea
Like the springs in a bed.

Michael Burton (7)
Baddow Hall Junior School

STORM

As fast as a bike crashing into a tree
As loud as 220 singers
As fast as a jet
As loud as a giant stomping
through the town
Like a baby crying in its cot
As powerful as 13 oxen
As wet as 4 rainstorms, one after another
As strong as an elephant picking up a tree
As cold as 10 freezers put together.

Lee Stopher (8)
Baddow Hall Junior School

RAIN

Rain sparkles like crystal
Falls like a bullet
Sounds like a gunshot
As it hits the ground
Makes massive puddles as
deep as the sea.
Splashes like stones
Is as miserable as someone
with no friends.

Joshua Bolton (8)
Baddow Hall Junior School

CATS

Cats' claws are like broken glass
Cats purr as quietly as a waterfall
Cats' paws as small as an apple
Fur as soft as a feather
Asleep they are as silent as rain
Awake they are as an owl at night.

Freddie Chatt (7)
Baddow Hall Junior School

SNOW

Snow like icing sugar
Falling like white paint on a clay lighthouse
Touching me like my white feather boa
Falls on the path like leaves in the wind
Soft like my cat's white bib
Can be shaped like melted chocolate.

Katy Matthewson (8)
Baddow Hall Junior School

DOG LIMERICK

There once was a lively dog - Rover
Who found a magical four-leafed clover
He kept it all day
Then finally came May
And he took it on holiday to Dover.

Caroline Evennett (10)
Barling Magna CP School

WIND

Wind is a mad monster destroying trees, cliffs and
everything in its path.
Wind is a monster truck, rampaging through the world
demolishing cliffs, houses and trees.
Wind is a nuclear missile firing its way through everything
above ground.
Wind is a mammoth tank tearing away everything living.
Wind is a Samurai sword thrashing and lurching
into the defenceless land.
Wind is a steam train thundering down the track
of trees and houses.
Wind is a steam vulture swooping down for its prey.

Tom Cuthell (11)
Barling Magna CP School

WIND

Wind is a man sprinting down
a track ripping up the grass behind him
Wind is a wolf destroying everything in its path
Wind is an angry bull pulling a tree up by its roots
Wind is a tractor tearing up the soil
Wind is a violent person shouting boldly at the trees
Wind is a hungry monster thumping on the ground ripping up trees
Wind is a hammer smashing down streets of houses.

Tasha Riley (11)
Barling Magna CP School

WIND

Wind is a ghost frightening all in its path
Wind is a knife slicing through the road
Wind is a flame scorching all the trees
Wind is a runaway train tearing down the street
Wind is a herd of wildebeests stampeding through
Wind is a cane punishing the mortal world
Wind is a pencil drawing fear and panic
Wind is a saw, sawing our hopes in two
Wind is a magnet repelling trees and homes.

Alexander Dowsett (10)
Barling Magna CP School

THE WIND

The wind is a tank crushing the leaves.
The wind is an owl swooping down
and picking up the litter.
The wind is a stealth jet sneaking up behind you,
then pushing you over.
Wind is a menace taking off your hat.
The wind is a granny screaming at the washing.
The wind is a giant trampoline on the houses.
Wind is a cat scratching at the trees.

Ben Crofts (10)
Barling Magna CP School

WIND

Wind is an angry wolf
howling at night.
Wind is a bad tempered man
screaming and shoving the leaves around.
Wind is a Tyrannosaurus-rex, stampeding through the wood.
Wind is a big bad monster, lifting the whole house up.
Wind is a protester, jumping on the world.
Wind is a vulture, tearing and destroying the branches.
Wind is a killer, taking people's houses away.
Wind is a power plant, blowing our solar system away.

Emily Sleigh-Johnson (10)
Barling Magna CP School

FROST

Frost is cold and freezing
I've begun sneezing
People are skating
but I'm just cold and waiting.
Frost is crystals melting away
He's like glittering stars,
and he freezes cars.
People are beginning to sneeze
and wheeze.
My hands are red raw and very sore.

Billy Jackson (11)
Barling Magna CP School

FROST

Frost is icicles hanging from trees
Frost is snow dripping on leaves
Frost is a pond frozen still
Frost is the cold, giving you a chill
Frost freezes boats even in the bay
I can't wait until another day.

Thomas Brambill (10)
Barling Magna CP School

FROST

Frost so clear and white
Crystal rivers sparkle bright
Water's still
Giving you a chill
Icicles hang from windowpanes
Children sliding down the lanes.

Gemma Batty (11)
Barling Magna CP School

FROST

Frost is a dagger hanging from a pane
Frost is a car, freezing in the lane
Frost is a knight, fighting for survival
Frost is now waiting for the sun's arrival
The sun comes out ready for battle
The frost is gone with a bit of a rattle!

Steven Sterry (10)
Barling Magna CP School

THE WIND

Wind is like a wild animal
tearing at the trees.
Wind is a racing car
racing past, blowing your hair.
Wind is like a mad man
blowing dust and litter everywhere.
Wind is a monster
ripping off roofs of houses.
Wind is an aeroplane swooping
round the world
Wind is like an angry tiger
chasing its prey.

Gemma Child (10)
Barling Magna CP School

WIND

Wind is an elephant smashing everything in its path
Wind is a wolf blowing rubbish around
Wind is a rhino knocking down trees
Wind is a jet, blowing kites about
Wind is a fast man blowing leaves in the air
Wind is a stampede smashing and crashing everything
Wind is a granny screaming for her umbrella.

Chris Humphrey (10)
Barling Magna CP School

RAIN

Rain splashing and splashing
trickling as it hits the ground.
People get damp, wet and soggy
and their boots get splodgy
Rain bubbles and gurgles and
taps at your window
When rain hits umbrellas
it drips and splashes on the ground.
Puddles are wet, soggy, cold and damp.

Leanne Jones (11)
Barling Magna CP School

LIMERICK

There was a young man from Dover
He had a young dog called Rover
He wished it was dead
So he hit its head
Then it was over - for Rover!

Sophie Holland (11)
Barling Magna CP School

LIMERICK

There once was a chicken called Ben
Who once got mistaken for a hen
He was insulted
And that resulted
In him turning into a wren!

Joe Storrar (11)
Barling Magna CP School

SUN

The sun is a yellow Frisbee
flying through the sky.

It is a yellow lifeboat
rushing through an outrageous sea.

The sun is a light bulb
against a blue and white room.

It is a golden earring
against a soft sky.

The sun is a twirl of paint
on a blue piece of paper.

Samantha Perry (10)
Barnes Farm Junior School

THE SUN

The sun is as shiny as a new coin

The sun glows as bright as catseyes
in the road.

The sun is as warm as an open log fire
on a cold winter's day.

The sun is as yellow as a newborn chick.

The sun is a big salami waiting to be cut.

Emma Simmonds (10)
Barnes Farm Junior School

SUN

The sun is a diamond ring dazzling in the light
The sun is a fire on the beach
The sun is a big spade in the sand
The sun is a big satsuma in the sky
The sun is some bright shoes.

Emily Hipgrave (11)
Barnes Farm Junior School

THINGS FOR THE MILLENNIUM

The millennium will be full of surprises
With celebrations and parties
It will be the year you will never forget
With the latest car designs
Modern technology and new computers
Games for children with 3D graphics
Things to help all schools
Soon you will be able to do your shopping with a click of a mouse
In the year 2000 a millennium playstation will be on sale
Cars will have televisions inside them
There will be a new fuel
And better roads
Soon tyres on cars will never lose air
Nations will not declare war against each other
On the 31st December 1999 midnight everybody will celebrate
People will buy pets
The fireworks make a lot of noise
People drink champagne and enjoy themselves
I can't wait until the millennium
Can you?

Chirag Desai (9)
Beehive Preparatory School

LOOKING FORWARD TO THE MILLENNIUM

We're all looking forward to the millennium,
After a thousand years we will be celebrating more,
Like more anniversaries,
and more computers for school.
We're all looking forward to the millennium,
It's going to be the year 2000,
lots of advanced technology,
and so much more.
There maybe new planets
in space,
There maybe things to help schools,
Even more equipment will still also do,
mostly it's a celebration to come soon.
Next year will be the millennium,
We're all looking forward to the next 1000 years.
Oh it will be great,
lots of fireworks going off,
there will lots of things to do.
There maybe flying school buses,
we do not know at all.
There will be lots more animals,
and much better laws.
Maybe there will be new buildings
and lots of sales too.
We may get things free,
there maybe new food,
probably new airlines.
We're all looking forward to the millennium,
way hey it's next year.

Vivek Gupta (8)
Beehive Preparatory School

NEW MILLENNIUM

There is a new millennium
On its way
We are waiting
Day by day.
We do not know
What the millennium will bring
Maybe it will bring
New poems to sing
Or maybe design
A new wedding ring.
There is a new millennium
On its way
We are waiting
Day by day
Will my computer go
I don't know!
There is a new millennium
On its way
We are waiting
Day by day.

Lauren Emma Shepherd (8)
Beehive Preparatory School

CELEBRATION PARTY

Celebration comes
In the year 2000.

We all have fun,
We are all happy.

So we celebrate,
Have a party.

Balloons are everywhere,
We put the music on.

We start to dance
And we have fireworks.
They make a loud noise,
Bang! Bang!

We all enjoy it,
It is very exciting.
We just love it
And we put everything on.

Even the television.
We just love the year 2000.
And when we go to bed,
We all dream about all the fun.

Surat Dhillon (9)
Beehive Preparatory School

HAPPY NEW YEAR!

Year 2000 comes to Earth,
Now it changes all the time,
Greetings to new toys and computers.
Now mums are happy because new shops arrive.
Oh my God, it's the millennium biro!
People making robots new,
They are called R2D2.
People having fun
With a millennium bun.
New space gravity is found,
Maybe Planet-X is a planet,
New space stuff is made.
We are going to party all night long until 2001!

Lucas Came (8)
Beehive Preparatory School

THE NEW MILLENNIUM

The new millennium is coming
And everything will be new.
There will be lots of exciting things happening
With lots of parties too!
There could be things to help some schools,
And new equipment and better tools.
New shops and better stores
And computer games so you won't get bored.
Designs for cars, with better roads,
Help helpless animals
And help the goats.
The fuel will be new and there will be better gas,
And the celebrating will come very fast.
It is almost time
For the millennium to come,
So let's get busy
And have some fun!

Erika Padua (8)
Beehive Preparatory School

How The Year 2000 Is Going To Be

I cannot wait until the year 2000.
It's going to be different.
The dates are going to change,
And all different things are going to happen.
We've still got eleven months,
I will be ten,
And my three other sisters
Are going to be twelve, fourteen and sixteen.
In our school, we are going to have new things, like
New sweets, gum, food and cakes.
Everything is going to change
And there may be people living on other planets,
With new space suits,
And on Mars, there could be shops and houses,
With space clothes.
I would like it.
Would you?

Annabel Singh (8)
Beehive Preparatory School

CELEBRATION

Celebration is first,
When the year 2000 comes.
It is very near.
The year 2000 is going to be special.
There will be more animals
And new looks, lots of parties,
People will have better cars and more games.
Balloons are everywhere,
People have their music on, celebrating.
All the people will be celebrating.
Everyone is enjoying themselves.
People love celebrating things
For the new millennium.

Hollie Cartwright (9)
Beehive Preparatory School

BIG BEN, MILLENNIUM IS HERE!

Big Ben, Big Ben, strike right now.
Big Ben, Big Ben, light up the town.
Big Ben, Big Ben, don't lose power.
Big Ben, Big Ben, don't wait one hour.
Big Ben, Big Ben, millennium is here.
Big Ben, Big Ben, let's get up and cheer.
Millennium, millennium come right now.
Millennium, millennium, come to my town.
Millennium, millennium, don't be late.
Millennium, millennium, come on the right date.
Millennium, millennium, you're right on time.
Millennium, millennium, everything is fine!

Samantha Rush (9)
Boreham Primary School

Two Thousand Years Ago . . .

A car, a bus, a train,
Two thousand years ago, none of this was the same.
You see an aeroplane flying by,
Two thousand years ago, it would have been a lie.
Planets, comets, galaxies and stars,
Two thousand years ago, people thought they were gods from afar.
You flick a switch, it turns on a light,
Two thousand years ago, it would have given them a fright.
People like to drink pop, eat burgers and chips,
Two thousand years ago, they mostly ate grapes with pips.
Today people worry, mostly about their looks,
Two thousand years ago, they worried about their sheep.
Have things changed that much? I don't know,
From Jesus' first day on Earth, two thousand years ago . . .

Timothy Reyland (11)
Boreham Primary School

When Year 2000 Comes

Time to wake up glittering sun,
1999 is on the run,
Year 2000 is drawing near,
So jump up high, shout and cheer.
Come along and get a seat,
Clap your hands,
And click your feet.
Time to wake up, glittering sun.

Sophie Wrigglesworth (9)
Boreham Primary School

TIME GOING PAST

Time, time flying so fast,
Celebrating people that have gone past.
Places, memories, happy and sad,
All the inventions that were good and bad.

Everybody likes to rock and dance,
Some people even like to prance,
A few people just like to wiggle,
And some just stand and start to giggle.

Time, time, years are going past,
I'm thinking about my future which I wish
would come fast,
I would like to be a football player and play
in the world cup
And score loads of goals in 2002 and go up.

Everybody likes to rock and dance,
Some people even like to prance,
A few people just like to wiggle,
And some just stand and start to giggle.

Matthew Watson (10)
Boreham Primary SchoolTick-Tock

TICK-TOCK,

The clock's not stopped.
Tock-tick,
It's coming so quick.
Only nine more months to go,
Tock-tick give it a kick.

The millennium's coming,
It's coming so fast,
But we must remember
Not to forget the past.

Tick-tock,
The clock's not stopped.
Tock-tick,
It's coming so quick.
Only nine more months to go,
Tock-tick give it a kick.

Saxons, Romans,
Normans, Tudors too,
All lived long before me and you.

Rebecca Martin (9)
Boreham Primary School

TIME CLICKING AWAY

Time, time, clicking away,
Flicking away slowly.
Ticking away every day,
The millennium is making its way.

So hurry!

Hurry, hurry, as quick as you can,
Come on, come on, millennium man!
There's cakes and jelly and ice-cream too,
But hurry, soon there'll be nothing for you.

So hurry!

It's fast, it's furious, it's coming this way,
Come on, come on, millennium day.
It's here, it's here, hip, hip hooray,
It's here, it's here, the millennium day.

Hooray!

Deborah Aitken (8)
Boreham Primary School

THE TWO THOUSANDTH YEAR

The two thousandth year is a special time,
While you sit at a table and dine.
You eat and drink,
And hardly blink,
While you listen to the clock chime.

What's the time?
It's half-past nine,
Only two and a half hours to go.
Doesn't time go so slowly?
Sleepily upstairs I climb.

While I sit in my bed,
Thinking in my head, why aren't I partying as well?
Laughing and playing,
Having so much fun,
Games to play for everyone.

One minute to twelve,
I just can't wait,
The year 2000 will be great.
Then the clock chimes,
Then I recline and fall asleep in my bed.

Anthony Nunez (11)
Boreham Primary School

THE MILLENNIUM DOME

The year two thousand is the best,
Its gleaming Dome is better than the rest.
If time capsules weren't there,
The great Dome would be bare.

The party is at twelve o'clock,
And I'm ready to rock!

The year two thousand is the best year,
Big men are having lots of beer!
People are in the hall,
We are all having a great ball.

The lights came on,
And my face shone.
Even people from Rome
Are having a great time,
In the Millennium Dome.

Thomas Nunez (8)
Boreham Primary School

THE YEAR TWO THOUSAND

The year two thousand is on the run.
What shall we do?
Let's have some fun!

The clock strikes twelve,
I can hear ringing bells.
It's the year two thousand, hip, hip hooray!
Now I had better stay!

The year two thousand is on the run.
What shall we do?
Let's have some fun!

Ringing bells in my ears,
Looking out of the window as everyone peers,
The millennium is coming up quick,
Listening in my head to the clock going tick.

The year two thousand is on the run.
What shall we do?
Let's have some fun!

Amy Westney (9)
Boreham Primary School

THE YEAR TWO THOUSAND IS THE BEST!

The year two thousand is the best,
It's number one, it beats the rest.
When the right time comes we'll start to eat,
And then get dancing,
Move those feet.

Step to the left,
Step to the right,
Keep on dancing
All through the night.

If you then think
The world will end,
You really must be round the bend.

Step to the left,
Step to the right,
Keep on dancing
All through the night.

But in a way, it won't last long,
But don't be wrong,
Don't be in tears,
Because there will be another one
In another thousand years.

Katy Reyland (8)
Boreham Primary School

TWO THOUSAND YEARS

I lie in bed wondering
Wondering about the world.
How old are the stars?
The moons? The clouds?
They must be older than two thousand years.

Two thousand years ago Jesus was born.
Kings followed that twinkling star,
Wearing their golden, silky cloaks,
Bearing their gifts from afar.
Then shivering, scared, the shepherds came
With their crooks up straight and high.
The star shone brightly, glowing above,
The angels sang in the sky.
And did Mary know what would happen to her son
During the years to come?

I lie in bed wondering.
Wondering about the world.
Are the same clouds, moons, stars,
Watching me in my life?
They must be older than two thousand years.

Rachel Andrew (10)
Boreham Primary School

MILLENNIUM STARS

Twinkling, twinkling, how old the stars are growing now,
They led Mary, Joseph, Jesus, but how?
Do they stay awake all night
To see such wonder and delight?
And when the morning has come,
Do they sparkle on the other side of the sun?
shining on babes so young,
A star to guide them, every one.
Our saviour was born in the dust and dirt,
At the dead of night,
But ended king of the Jews.
This doesn't seem right.
Children now are born
In comfy, warm beds with tender care.
Now being born
Is strange and very rare.
Boys and girls have been born,
Every day for thousands of years.
Sleeping at night, stars peep into windows,
To collect bedtime tears.
All that time of loyal protection,
What do they get back from us upon this special year?
Two thousand years, two thousand stars,
All kissed by little children that night.
The stars start slowly winking out to sleep,
So close your eyes tightly for what is yet to come,
Welcome, welcome, welcome, millennium!

Zoe Copson (10)
Boreham Primary School

MY MILLENNIUM

Men and women rush around,
Their feet don't even touch the ground.
In their cars going very fast, polluting the air,
They don't really seem to care.
For goodness sake, slow down I say,
There really could be another way.
The 21st century I want to see,
Splendid creatures and magnificent trees.
I want to keep the air that we breathe
Clean and pure so all life forms are secure.
Let's end all wars and live together,
Within nature's world, forever.

Amelia Burns (9)
Boreham Primary School

2000

There's fun parties every day,
People are cheering on their way,
Music and dancing,
Discos are here,
I think the millennium is oh so dear.
The parties are so inviting,
I think they're going to be exciting
We will dance 'til dawn.
The next day, we will
Definitely be yawning!
I think the millennium is drawing near!

Fuschia Burgess (9)
Boreham Primary School

Rock, Millennium's Here!

Rock! Rock!
Millennium's here.
How long will it take, a year?
Two days, three days or a week?
Should I have a little peek?

Rock! Rock!
Jump up and down!
It's millennium all around.
No one would dare to make a frown,
Too happy,
Jump up and down!

Rock! Rock!
All my friends are here,
One, two, three,
And we are getting ready to cheer,
Millennium's here.

Sarah Clements (9)
Boreham Primary School

The Year 2000

The millennium is here,
The clock is ticking,
And we're going to have a party.
It's going to be fun.
The year 2000 is so great,
The day is starting to go,
I've had such fun,
But now it's time to go.

Siân Rice (9)
Boreham Primary School

ROCK TO THE MILLENNIUM POP

Grooving, grooving,
Even more moving,
Rock 'til you drop,
Even more pop!

Jump over here,
Jump over there,
Glare at the girls,
I don't care!

Grooving, grooving,
Even more moving,
Rock 'til you drop,
Even more pop!

I'm going home,
Very sad,
All the memories,
Good and bad.
I know it's hard to leave the gang!

Grooving, grooving,
Even more moving,
Rock 'til you drop,
Even more pop!

Christopher Hills (8)
Boreham Primary School

THE YEAR 2000 IS GREAT

The year 2000's going to be great,
I don't care if it's early or late,
It will be fun,
And everyone will come!

People dancing everywhere,
Singing happily as they dare,
Spinning around and then can't stop,
Happily moving like Top of the Pops.
Grinning faces, smiling at me,
Celebrating night and day.

The year 2000's going to be great,
I don't care if it's early or late,
It will be fun,
And everyone will come!

Hannah Mace (8)
Boreham Primary School

THE MAGIC BOX

I will put in my box,
Lots of golden chocolate to eat,
A teddy, singing lovely songs at night,
A tornado, spinning round in circles,
Breaking everything in sight,
The Spice Girls singing all day and never stopping,
The teacher always teaching,
She carries on all day and night, and you
Can never get her to stop.

Sarah Robinson (8)
Earls Hall Junior School

DREAMS

I was locked in my room,
Through the night.
Even through the day,
I was locked in so I couldn't play.
People screaming, I wasn't dreaming.
My dreams twisting in and out of my eyes,
I was falling from great heights,
Hitting buildings whilst falling through the air.
Why me? It wasn't fair.
There were cries of people I used to know,
There were cries of ghosts that were killed in
The deadly, white snow.
Now I'm back in my own soft bed,
You've got to say at least,
I'm not dead.

Clare Campbell (9)
Earls Hall Junior School

LOST IN SPACE

It was prowling, prowling,
hungry as a wolf.
My spine turns to jelly,
crying like a baby, I just want to go home.
There is a screaming,
it has pounced.
Dead as a doornail,
as wild as a bat.
It is watching me like a hawk.
A flash of light blinds me.
It has gone.

Jack Lidster-Woolf (8)
Earls Hall Junior School

WAR

His hair was made of strands of blood,
and greasy trench mud.
He wears trousers with bullet holes
as big as watch faces, and a
camouflage jacket of pain.
He would eat flesh and the organs
of dead soldiers.
His teeth are like the bones of war heroes.
His breath smells like the sea of
mustard gas that surrounds them.
He lives with the death of his soldiers
and he feels the war will never end.
He sleeps in terror and fright,
waiting for the sound of the gun shells.
And even when it's all over,
he is still listening for the sound of death.
This enemy is his past,
it's ruining his life like the army did.

Sarah Edwards (11)
Earls Hall Junior School

A TRIP INTO OUTER SPACE

A trip into outer space,
Spaceships having a humungous race,
Blasting guns, bullets everywhere,
Spaceships flying here and there.
Astronauts scared out of their wits,
Spaceships blasting intergalactic families to bits.
Some are silly families, aliens do not have friends,
Spaceships go round very big bends.

Gregory Moulton (9)
Earls Hall Junior School

WAR

Her gory locks are a mixture of blood and
strands of dirt and filth.
She wears a gown of barbed wire and
nightmares, twisted together.
Her face is red with blood and she has scars
where pieces of shrapnel are embedded in her cheeks.
Her eyes are wild and frightened.
She feeds on the thick, black, heavy, clouds of smoke,
gulping it down, hungrily.
Her teeth are rotten and falling out
of her bleeding, swollen, gums.
Her breath is putrid and smells of disease and death.
She lives in the cold, wet, muddy trenches dug by men.
She sleeps in a large pit.
her blankets are the corpses of dead soldiers,
and her pillow is a gun.
She dreams of lost friends that will
never share her life again.
Her children are the fighting and pain
who follow her eagerly.
Her enemy is peace and health and happiness.

Miriam Nicholas (11)
Earls Hall Junior School

THE RAMPAGING WIND

The rampaging wind goes everywhere,
Confusing people where it will scare.
It goes to the house tops rumbling away.
It scares people now, which way it will rain.
It goes down your chimney pot, moaning away.
Now it even scares Father Christmas away!

Gary Derbridge (9)
Earls Hall Junior School

WAR

Her hair is made from a thousand bodies
laying side by side on the ancient battlefield.
Her face is scarred by the bullets from the enemy's guns.
Her ebony teeth are grotesquely uneven, like a town
after it has been hit by a hundred bombs.
Her breath is like hundreds of decomposing corpses,
from fifty years ago.
She wears a dress made from the blood of her dead enemies.
She eats the remains of the enemy and
drops their souls into the flames of hell!
She lives in the trenches, metres into the ground.
She dreams about watching the wars that have been.
Her children are the armies that will fight future wars.
She wants to stop the enemy gaining land
that is not rightfully theirs.
Her enemies are the armies who try to
kill her children and take her land.

Kerry-Ann Jervis (10) & Rachel Mundy (11)
Earls Hall Junior School

THE SNAKE

A snake slithered through the grass,
so silent, smooth, none heard her pass.

Her nest she seeks her head to lay,
in rest again to end her day.

Her eggs she sees and curls up tight,
to sleep again through another night.

Holly Dixon (10)
Earls Hall Junior School

THE RIVER

I am the river, I have no friends and I am lonely.
I wear the mud which holds me in place.
My hair is the cold air.
My face looks like floating frogspawn.
I eat smelly, small fish.
My teeth are the cobblestones that lie at
the bottom of the lake.
I live in the mountains,
I sleep in the lake.
I dream about going into the clouds.
My children are seaweed,
I most want to evaporate into the air.
My enemies are the children that swim there.

Daryl Bush (9)
Earls Hall Junior School

WAR

His hair is men's shoelaces.
His combat jacket is the gloom of darkness.
His trousers are the fear of death.
His face is like something out of a horror film.
His teeth are mud-coated.
His breath is the fire,
sweeping through the battlefield.
He sleeps in the wreck of an armoured car.
He dreams about shell-shocked men.
His children are the pieces of shrapnel
from the bombers, piercing the flesh of men.
He lives in the legendary poppy.

Russell Taylor (11)
Earls Hall Junior School

ALIEN ON EARTH

Alien on the earth, alien at the seaside, alien in the homes
The alien goes everywhere. The alien comes to tea.
Everyone is scared except for me. The alien is nice except to me.
I have nowhere to go but the alien can.
I went to the shop, the alien came with me and ate me for tea.
Where did he come from? Nobody knows.
How did he get here? Nobody knows.
When we all found out he was eating the ground
He said to me ''Where's tea?'
Alien on Earth, alien on Earth.
Everybody knows except for me.
He ate Mum so now she is dead.
A different alien said to my friend
'Would you like to be me?
Come in my spaceship to have some tea.'
I said 'No.' He said 'Yes, please come with me.'
I said 'OK.' He said 'No.'
But you said I could. 'OK then.'

Chelsie Lewis (9)
Earls Hall Junior School

ALIENS

We were floating in space
When a big, bad alien
Used lasers to shoot at us.
We landed on squidgy Mars.
We met friendly aliens,
Sang 'Hey Diddle Diddle',
And the bad alien
Crashed into the sun.

Ben Allen (9)
Earls Hall Junior School

WINTER PERSONIFICATION POEM

His name is the chilling sound of the wind whistling
through the leafless trees.
His hair is the wool that keeps us warm in the winter.
For his clothes he wears the white blanket of snow which
envelopes the cold floor.
His face is as smooth as a snowflake that fell to the ground
in the first winter.
Winter's teeth are the icicles that hang like
transparent stalactites from roofs of buildings.
He is as old as the Earth which began before life started.
Winter white is the colour that he relishes and enjoys.
He has an enemy called Summer, with the colour of sun; yellow,
who is hot, unlike him.
He has one friend who respects him.
Spring is his friend though there is no snow at that time of year.
He has a wife named Autumn who is also like a best friend
as Autumn is the closest season to winter.
His hobby is seeing how much cold white snow he can
cover the Earth with.
He sleeps on the whistling trees and the soft clouds
awaiting next winter.
He dreams about the icy covering Jack Frost has laid.
He lives at the end of the year when Winter
starts all over again,
And dies at the end of the year when his
enemy (Summer) starts to brew.

Amanda Coban (10)
Earls Hall Junior School

A TRIP INTO SPACE

A trip into space,
Some aliens having a race,
They run so quick,
And they're being sick.
What are they going to do next?

Why not come and join us for dinner,
So then you will get much thinner.

They eat people and animals
And ride on camels,
And then they go to bed,
But then wake up to bang their heads.

How stupid!

When they're ready to go to school,
They go down the crooked hall.
They learn about us,
Then they're making a fuss
When are they going to stop!

Emma Howell (8)
Earls Hall Junior School

ALIEN'S HOLIDAY

We're going along in our spaceship
us aliens with four eyes.
We are setting off very slowly
eating alien pies!

We'll soon hit Earth
humans, cars, buildings and all.
We will then be on holiday
swimming in a swimming pool.

We will go to the beach and eat some ice-cream.
We'll then have to go home
(but my brother doesn't want to)
so he will scream.

Frances Morris (9)
Earls Hall Junior School

ICICLES

Her hair is the silky, clear water dripping from her
domed head.
She's aged for hundreds of years, though she looks young
and free.
Smelling of fresh morning dew from April showers
drip dropping off the tips of bright, green leaves.
She frequently hears the constant whistle of the wind.
Her favourite colour, translucent white - her and her friends.
Her hobby is to lounge in the frosty cave,
dripping with water onto the slippery floor.
Her home, along with thousands of other icicles, is the dark,
wet cave that seems to go on for eternity.
Her nickname is Head Point as her head seems
the sharpest of them all.
Her friends are the snow and frost that help her
exist that little bit longer.
Her children are the miniature icicles that seem
to be glued to her.
She wasn't born; she began life when there was a
massive storm hundreds of years ago.
Her enemy, the sun, with splintering heat in the mid-summer.

Claire Walsh (11)
Earls Hall Junior School

PERSONIFICATION POEM

His hair is made of thick black dust
He wears torn old foul-smelling clothes
which have not been washed for weeks.
His face looks black with terror but
his grey long greasy hair just covers his scar.
He eats what he can find throughout
the dark streets of London.
His teeth are broken, rotting like bones
in a grave.
His breath is like a breath of
five thousand chillies.
He lives in a bombed, cold, damp, wet
Anderson shelter and he sleeps in a
horrid hair-raising shack.
He dreams about bombing and the
death of his children and he dreams
of nightmares he will never forget.
His children are lost in time
and his enemy is death, death and more death.

Mark Howell (10)
Earls Hall Junior School

IT'S A . . .

Planet controller,
Unidentified mover,
Terrible handwriter,
Ugly creature,
Spaceship rider,
Earth attacker,
Sky flyer . . .
           Alien.

Sophie Costello & Theresa Jackson (10)
Earls Hall Junior School

ME AND THE TIGER

The tiger is big and brave and bold,
he's very fierce, or so I'm told.

To find his food, he goes out at night
And all other animals shake with fright.

I do not think I'd like to see
the tiger looking straight at me.

So, perhaps it's best I stay at home
and in the jungle he can roam.

Or, I could always go with you
and see a tiger in the zoo.

Daniel Humphrey (9)
Earls Hall Junior School

THE WATERFALL

The rain falls on the ground,
Splashing and spitting in the full drains.
The water goes drip, drip, drip,
The water swishes up and down it goes.
Water stays and goes.
The sun comes out and the rain goes again.
The thunder crashes, the rain comes down.
The alien came down from the big world.
He had eight big eyes,
He had six legs.
He had three ears on the top of his head.

Sandy Wilson (9)
Earls Hall Junior School

WINTER POEM

Her hair would be made of warm dripping icicles.
She would wear a long snowflake dress down to her ankles.
Her shoes made of ice
Face of a cloud
Her eyes are rain on a winter's day.
She would have frosted lips
She would eat snowstorms every night and snow geese.
Her teeth as snowdrops
Her breath smells like the wind on a cold day.
She lives in a snowball house with snowflakes in her house.
She sleeps in a snowberry bed that is warm.
She dreams about the next day.
Her children have snow clothes.
She has 10 children and they have rain eyes like their mum.
She wants to have a big, big snow house and lots of money.
Her enemy is the Snow Queen and the Snow Queen's helpers.

Charlotte Gray (10)
Earls Hall Junior School

THE ALIEN

There were two flying spaceships going very slow
Then eight little aliens waved out of a big window
Suddenly in the moonlight someone was beamed up into space
Then I saw an alien's really ugly face.

It had four humungous eyes
That gave me a huge surprise
The next night I stared out the window
And spotted it all again.

But this time in the spaceship there were now ten.
After a while it landed in my back yard.
The alien came to the window with a big card.
He went back to h is spaceship

And zoomed into space.
I thought I saw him land on the moon
And go back to his base.

Abigail Mitchell (9)
Earls Hall Junior School

PERSONIFICATION POEM - JACK FROST

His hair is made of bright, white, morning dewdrops,
dripping down his face.
His teeth are made of icicles as cold as the Antarctic
with points as sharp as knives' blades.
His children are the snowflakes which float
lightly down from Heaven.
The sun, his enemy, he despises. She melts the
frost he leaves down to a solution.
Down in hell, with the devil he sleeps. Out at night
he comes, nocturnal he lives, daylight to him is night.
Covering the world in thick frost one night,
in his complete fantasy.
Snow, his friend, he helps a lot. Together they
work to make the world cold.
A fresh minty scent, is his type of fragrance,
he applies it at night.
Fog, his partner. Together two villains.
They don't make life easy for mortals.
Black, he loves, to him it shows bleakness.
He will live on forever, to eternity and will still
be here when the world ends.

Sarah Matthew (11)
Earls Hall Junior School

WAR

His hair is like sizzling fuses advancing closer and closer
before exploding on the battlefield.

He would wear a long jacket of bright red poppies and
trousers that will be bloodstained for all eternity.

His face sooty and scarred while his grenade-like eyes
darted from side to side staring at what he had created.

He would eat the sabotaged countries with the lifeless
soldiers lying upon them.

His teeth are the twisted bullets that have killed
whole regiments.

His breath smells like the odour of decaying soldiers
lying in the war-zone.

War lives in all the dead bodies that have fought
in the war.

He sleeps in a sulphurous, sunless and sinister place
where no one has been before.

He dreams about weapons firing into the air.
His children are all the lifeless troops lying in the
dingy, wet, muddy trenches.

He most wants to get every country in the world
to go into war.

His enemies are all the countries who want
to make peace.

Robert Keane & Alan Archer (11)
Earls Hall Junior School

WIND

His hair would be made of raindrops which have fallen
from the sky.
Wearing grey, fluffy clouds he would prance around the air.
He smells of the sea air splashing in the waves.
Snowflakes are his favourite meal, melting on his tongue.
His favourite colour is white like the colour of mist.
At night he assists Jack Frost put ice on all the cars.
In summer he dreams about winter and all the cold nights
soon to come.
His age nobody knows though he is ever living.
His children are the icicles frozen on the buildings.
His enemy is heat making the world hot.

Sarah Marshall (11)
Earls Hall Junior School

WAR

His hair would be like blood-curdled jackets from dead troops
who fought for their country.
He would wear skulls and bones from deceased soldiers
stitched together by the needle of hope.
His eyes are fixed and dilated like a lifeless corpse on his death-bed
and he is scorched and scarred by the grenades of his enemy.
He would eat dead men's souls and drop them at the gates of Heaven.
His teeth would be red from the blood-red poppies growing in the field.
His breath would smell putrid from the decomposed dead bodies
in the battlefield.
His home is the battlefield where it is always dense midnight.
He would live in oily, waterlogged, dingy trenches.

Hannah Brown & Blair Wilson (10)
Earls Hall Junior School

THE OCEAN KING

The ocean king has no hair.
He wears two fins and a fish tail.
He is half fish and half man.
He eats children who step near the ocean.
All his teeth have fallen out.
His breath is nice because he is in the ocean.
He lives on the outside of the ocean.
He sleeps in the middle of the ocean.
He has nightmares of pretty things like flowers.
He has other family that live in the other oceans,
But his children live in the sea.
He wants to see his children.
The land is his enemy.

Suzanna Scott (10)
Earls Hall Junior School

PERSONIFICATION POEM

His hair is made of fear and sadness.
He wears the bones of soldiers that fight.
His face is like a dying meadow.
His teeth are like pieces of broken wire.
He sleeps in the ruins of the houses.
His children are the shells of bombs.
His enemies are the good and kind.

Rachel Norrington (10)
Earls Hall Junior School

THE WAR

The straightness of her hair is converted into metal bars,
She would wear an uncomfortable ragged cloak with a
                         drenched petticoat underneath,
Her face would look bruised and clattered,
She would eat mouldy half-eaten grouse,
Her teeth would crack and crumble through the agony of chewing,
Her breath would make you think of a roaring cannonball shooting
                                   out of her mouth,
She would only just about have a roof covering her head,
Her bed would be passed away plants and animals,
She dreams of the banging and bleeding of people being shot,
Her enemy would be the dark scary sky and mist which would
                              make her shiver.

Amy Andrews (9)
Earls Hall Junior School

THE LONELY LAND

This distinguished island in a lonely land,
Set me to thinking this was a lonely island.
The remarkable animals and plants,
Were colours you only imagine in your dreams.
The animals were not scared to come out.
They would even let me touch them, with no fear in sight.
The plants were just swaying in the breeze.
How I got there -
I was looking for my mysterious friend.
I walked along the rocky shore and found him there.

Laura Kent (10)
Earls Hall Junior School

THIS IS WHAT HE REALLY IS

His hair is made of metal pipes and dead people's bones.
The clothes which he would wear are broken glass and strands
of kidneys.
The face of this man would be explosive guns shooting.
This man would wear old smelly clothes which had blood all over them.
His teeth would be covered in mud with blood and grass all over
the gums.
His breath is mustard gas. Anyone who went near him would die
in an instant.
He would live in the Mediterranean sea in a blacked-out old cave.
He would sleep in a battlefield or in a non-silent road.
His dreams are about someone who would take him away to a
deserted island.
His children are dead people's bodies and horse manure.
This man's greatest ambition is to be a normal person who never dies.
The enemy is the Nazi party and the atomic bomb.

Emma Archer (9)
Earls Hall Junior School

THE ISLAND JOURNEY

I wake up in the morning,
and get ready for a long trek along the island,
treading across sand which makes my feet sink
and the sea which gushes up to my feet.
I see birds' nests and seagulls squawking,
I see the calm flowing sea and large coconuts grow.
I wish that I could have a cool swim
and explore the treasures underneath.
I climb the rocks which are like stepping stones,
and think to myself what a day it's been.

Lucy Golding (9)
Earls Hall Junior School

The Deserted House

As you requested, I rode to that eerie house in Blackthorn forest.
There was deadly silence, not a sound.
As Blackie (my horse) stood chomping the grass,
I boldly walked forward and smote upon the door.
There were rainbow streaks dancing around in front of me.
Then I cried into the frosty air, 'Is anyone there? Anyone at all?'
I felt in my heart their strangeness, as if there were phantom listeners.
Then I called out with the last of my strength,
'Tell them I came, tell them I kept my word.'
Then I slowly stepped back and jumped upon my black stallion
And galloped into the starry distance.

Catrina Miles (9)
Earls Hall Junior School

War

His hair is made out of trembling fear,
And his clothes a blood-bath, evil and despair.
His face would look like the father of death.
He would eat some bloodthirsty animal or person.
His teeth are made out of blood of children
And his breath would smell like man's blood and smoke.
He lives in the palace of death.
He sleeps in a bed covered with thorns.
His children are also the children of death.
His greatest wish is to conquer the world.
His enemy is happiness
And his friend is sadness.

Madeeha Rafiq (9)
Earls Hall Junior School

WAR

His mane is the cringing screeches of bombs and the gory landing,
He wears the flattened houses in the industrial cities of England.
His face is the white baby in the dark blackout.
He eats the wounded army's supplies and the sad world's rations.
His teeth are the sharp bullets the army carry with them.
His house is the most powerful war camp.
His body covers the whole campsite when he lays to rest.
He dreams about the painful sound of the blitz siren.
His children are the poppies who lived long after him.
His enemy is peace that stays in terrified and worried people's hearts.

Hannah Lynch (10)
Earls Hall Junior School

WAR

Her hair would be like strands of sadness
She would wear a ragged dress full of death and poison
Her face would be drowning in sorrow
She would consume and digest all deathly things
Her breath would be like the smell of fear
She would live in an old wrecked building
She would rest in the fire of hell
She would dream about soldiers fighting at war
Her children are lonely with nowhere to go
She wants to rule the world
Her enemy is love, friendship and peace.

Laura Rayner (9)
Earls Hall Junior School

WAR

Her strands of hair are cruel and sad.
They are depressing, they barge through happiness.
She wears rags, plain and thin.
Her face is dirt-covered, never been washed.
It has an expression of hope though.
She survives on bread and a drop of water.
Never will she have lots to eat.
Her teeth are coated in agony, with blood all over her gums.
Her breath is the smoke from fires, never being put out.
She lives in death and cruelty.
She sleeps in the wreck of a burned plane.
Her children are death and grieving,
They will never be joyous or pleased.
She wishes she could end all fights.
Her enemy is her cruel cold self.
She wishes she could die with the soldiers,
And mourns for them each day.
Her effect will live on forever,
As she is eternal.

Christine Dutton (10)
Earls Hall Junior School

THE MAGIC BOX

The sound of Christmas golden bells,
Golden chocolate, sparkling green trees.
A bucket full of sparkling water,
A very big sea which is very strong.
The tweet tweet of birds,
Trembling, rain thundering.
Lightning flashing all at once,
People's pencils scratching as they work.

Natalee Bailey (8)
Earls Hall Junior School

His . . .

His hair is made from bits of bars
and frightful thrills.
He wears rags of sewn blankets.
His face has pieces of glass and blisters
that look and feel like bombs blowing up tiny houses.
He would eat spaghetti that slithers like snakes
and sauce like people's blood and cries.
His teeth are like houses' roofs falling from gas bombs.
His breath is like fires and smoke from streets and cities.
He lives in city dumps and smells of gutters.
He sleeps in agony in old shelters from World War I.
He dreams of pencil-chewing in his mouth.
At night and every night his kids are like
tickings of clocks, watches and bells.
He wants to be furious, he wants to
kill, kill, I say kill!
His enemies are the killing monsters from Germany.
This is the *end* of the world!

Graeme Riches
Earls Hall Junior School

Exquisite Corpse

Spotty animals exchanging a pound for sweets.
The smelly shelf running a race.
An excellent toilet pouring the elephant down it.
The good ruler sends kisses.
A skateboarding crazy box.
The stinky book hopping around.
People roller-skating like birds.
A fantastic tummy that can fly.
The silly pig that can fly in the sky.

Elizabeth Winter (8)
Earls Hall Junior School

WAR

Her gruesome, straggly hair is a substance of fear, hatred and death.
Her ragged dress is covered in blood and poison.
Her face is hideous with bombs for eyes.
Her lips are a mixture of sorrow and pain.
She has a scar of a skull on her upper lip.
She feeds on the flesh and souls of heroic GIs.
Her teeth are like mouldy bread and shaped like bombshells.
Her breath is sour, grotesque and despair, it's gas.
She lives in the decayed bodies of men.
She sleeps in the fire of hell.
She dreams a dream that says she will win.
Her children are despair, hatred, sorrow, death and pain.
She wants to prove she will survive and live forever.
Her enemies are peace, harmony, love, kindness and happiness.

Natalie Ford (10)
Earls Hall Junior School

PERSONIFICATION POEM

His hair is made of the sadness of the war.
He wears a gleaming suit.
His teeth are like an old apple.
His breath smells of rotten blood.
He lives in an underground tunnel.
He sleeps in a dirt tray.
His worst enemy is Germany.
He flies through the night.
He eats what he can find.
He dreams of being with his family.

Frankie Moss (9)
Earls Hall Junior School

WAR

Her hair was made of gruesome doom
and death upon her will.
She would wear an outfit of starvation
and shouting screams of death.
Her face is like a child's with a dress
as frilly as can be, and the look of sadness
on every evacuee.
She would eat bloodstained clothes
and bombs of every shape and size.
Her breath is the smell of death
and the smell of a gas mask.
She lives in the blackout and in smoke
from a gas bomb.
She sleeps in air raid shelters
and in the fire of death.
She dreams of soldiers fighting
the battle against war.
Her children are pain and sorrow
from soldiers at war.
Her enemy is happiness, love and peace.

Jenny Fidgeon (9)
Earls Hall Junior School

PRETTY BEAR

Pretty bear swimming round
Trying not to make a sound.
Catching fish all day long,
Beautiful bear in the river and sea,
Let's go home, it's time for tea.

Harriet Tindell (8)
Earls Hall Junior School

PERSONIFICATION POEM

His name is Jack Frost.
His hair is the Arctic slippery icicles.
He wears the snowflakes which become the frost on the grass.
Like Peter Pan he stays childlike and *never* grows up.
He lives under the cool, cool ground when the sun comes out,
But when the dew is down he appears and creates the frost.
His wife is Mrs Jack Frost and when Mr Frost is gone she creates
                              the frost for Mr Jack Frost.
His favourite colour is the white, white frost which his wife creates
                              when he's gone.
His breath is the mist which has no odour.
His children are the frost that his wife creates while he's gone.
He plays games with his children, playing the games he loves doing.
His enemy is the shining red hot sun,
For he melts his family.

Helen Illman & Theresa Jackson (10)
Earls Hall Junior School

THE MAGIC BOX

Golden sugar mouse.
Golden apples on a silver chocolate tree.
Fire rod lit up into bright colours.
The sparkle of silver water.
Fireworks lit up and banging.
The bright sun going down is a nice orange.
The sparkle of silver water glittering in the night.
Fireworks light up and bang in the night.
The bright sun going down in nice orangey colours
Saying hello to the moon.

Jessica Bekir (8)
Earls Hall Junior School

WAR

His hair was full of eyes.
He wore clothes and his trousers were full of spiders.
His face was like a tomato.
He would eat spiders and ants.
His teeth were like a banana's.
His breath was like steaming fire.
He lives in a shattered old house.
He sleeps in a tent.
He dreams about dragons.
His children were Sharon and Adam.
He wanted to sleep all day and night.
His enemy was a crocodile because he smells.

Scott McEwan (9)
Earls Hall Junior School

WAR

His hair was made of bits of old bones,
He would wear the flesh of those who rest,
His face was hideous and full of fear,
He eats the pain and suffering of others,
His teeth are like mud and rust,
His breath was made of gas and smoke,
He lives deep, deep underground,
He sleeps in a dump full of rats,
He dreams of killing others,
His children are his gun and sword,
His ambition is to kill!
His enemies are the non-followers.

Ben Fraser (9)
Earls Hall Junior School

MY BEST FRIEND

My best friend is Chris.
He plays nice games with me.
I invite him round my house.
We play on my Super Nintendo.
He invites me round his house.
We play in his garden.
We play football.
We make up.
Sometimes he holds his cheeks
And pulls them open and smiles.
He is the best.
He is my only best friend.
He is kind to me.
He is really friendly to me.
He will never let me down.

Alex Segrave (8)
Earls Hall Junior School

HOW TO MAKE AN ELEPHANT

Ears as floppy as a cloth.
A trunk as sucking as a Hoover.
Hair as spiky as a hedgehog.
Legs as long as logs.
Tail as short as a whip.
Eyes as black as shadows.
Chin as spiky as a pin.
A tongue as short as a worm.
Lips as fat as a pencil case.

Rachel Dale (8)
Earls Hall Junior School

THE WIND

The wind twirls the leaves around from the trees
and hears the children say *'Whee!'*
Hear the wind howl from distance,
hear the wind howl from near.
When you hear the wind howl
it disturbs your study.
You'd best wrap up warm otherwise
you'll *atishoo, atishoo,* get a cold like me.
The wind blows me everywhere,
make your mind up, you're giving me a scare.
The wind is making a stormy night,
no one likes it because it gives them a fright.
He breaks chimney pots from different spots,
now it's coming to a low wind, that's the end of this poem.

Danny Craig (9)
Earls Hall Junior School

SADNESS FEELS LIKE . . .

Sadness is blue like tears in your eyes,
Smells like ocean snails,
Tastes like freezing salty water,
Feels like stones hitting your back,
Looks like shocking waves,
Sounds like whales.

Racheal Bennion (10)
Earls Hall Junior School

GENERAL WIND

The weatherman said this wind you should dread
For this wind is strong and interminable.
It gave the lady a frightful scare by the wind
          that goes just everywhere.
As birds try to fly, all they do is get blown and
          thrown about.
What a problem for Tony Blair, 'Where shall I go,
          where, where?'
It gives everyone a terrible scare, the trees are branches
          everywhere.
What a bluster, what a cluster.
All this blast, all thanks to General Wind.

Brian Lindoe (9)
Earls Hall Junior School

THE GROWLING LION

In March the lion was growling,
Down the chimney pots there was a horrid howling,
There was no heat, only a beat,
Outside it was so gusty.
The wind made my house dusty,
But everybody says he is never kind,
The wind didn't have a single mind,
The wind was sure tough,
The people hated the wind's puff,
I'm very sure he'll rise again
And floods our streets with striking rain!

Sophie Wilson (9)
Earls Hall Junior School

THE MARCH WIND

In March, the angry lion was growling,
Down the chimney pots there was a horrible howling.
He is everywhere, except in the school,
He's even in the pool playing with a ball!
People believe he is good, while others say he is bad,
He blows down the chimney pots and even froze the baby's cot!
But don't worry, he will go away when the summer comes.
He will be a little lamb!

Adam Loveridge (9)
Earls Hall Junior School

THE WINDY NIGHT

One windy night when the wind was howling,
It went echoing through the streets and blowing
                                 down the lanes,
Rattling the latches and banging at the windowpanes.

Lucy Armstrong (8)
Earls Hall Junior School

EXQUISITE CORPSE

The dotty porridge was jumping with an ugly knife.
The smelly dog was kicking a stripy gun.
The stinky potion was playing with a dwarfy toilet.
The amazing computer swimming in smelly socks.
A wobbly zebra playing silly ant.

Francesqua Bragg (8)
Earls Hall Junior School

TEN LITTLE CHILDREN

Ten little children standing in a line,
A car came and ran over one
And then there were nine.
Nine little children going to space,
One fell off the rocket
And then there were eight.
Eight little children in a car to Spain,
One fell off and then there were seven.
Seven little children on a lolly to the North Pole,
One froze to death
And then there were six.
Six little children on a helicopter to Mexico,
One fell off
And then there were five.
Five little children sitting on a wall,
One fell off
And then there were four.
Four little children in school,
One got sent out
And then there were three.
Three little children in a desert,
Along came a scorpion, stung one
And then there were two.
Two little children going to England on an aeroplane,
One fell off and then there was one.
One little child got eaten by an alien,
Then there were none.
No little children - can't do anything.

Ryan Williams (8)
Earls Hall Junior School

WHILST WAITING AT THE HAIRDRESSERS

Whilst waiting at the hairdressers
There are all these horrible hairspray smells as you walk
In (not a nice welcome).

Whilst waiting at the hairdressers
There are chairs with big bumps in them from the person
Who was there before.

Whilst waiting at the hairdressers
There are nylon gowns that stick to you and your hair
Falls down your neck.

Whilst waiting at the hairdressers
There are shavers that tickle the back of your neck and
The scissors nearly cut your ears off. Ouch!

Next please!

After my haircut
The hairdresser makes a fuss of me
And I watch my brother go next!

David Smith (10)
Frinton-On-Sea Primary School

LIGHT

When light is there it is bright and everyone is happy.
Light is brilliant, everyone likes light,
Starlight glows with a gentle gleam,
Torches flare with rays of light,
Lanterns glow with a candle inside.

Bulbs shine in lighthouses,
Glass sparkles in the sun,
All is dark without light,
Lamps give us light as well as beacons.

Flashes of light give off a gleam,
Without light, nobody is happy,
Without light everything is dark,
Light is cheerful and makes people thankful.

Everybody should be grateful for the sun and
everything that produces light.
Flint makes light with a glint.

Liam Battersby (10)
Frinton-On-Sea Primary School

DO YOU WANT TO COME ROUND MINE?

Do you want to come round to mine? Oh let's go to yours,
Follow me, I'm right behind you,
I'll get you a chair, you can sit on the floor,
It doesn't matter where you sit, my mum or dad are sure to spit.

I'll put your food out for the dustman to collect,
So you'll run after him, you must be quick,
I'll bend the spoon to make it straight,
You can be the rest of the bait,
I'll cut my hair to make it long
And I'll get in the bath and I'll get so very dirty.

I'll wear some clothes that are so dirty, they're clean,
I will put this rubbish in the non bin basket,
I'll swim in ever so dry water,
I'll run so fast I'm going slow,
I'll lie somewhere comfortable, so I'll lie on the floor.

Ross George Lilley (10)
Frinton-On-Sea Primary School

LIGHT, DARK

Dark

Creaking of the floorboards
as footsteps are heard and
the wind whistles outside,
The trees are swaying
as the window
Shatters.
The owl hoots
in the garden and
Shuffling is heard,
soon, silence
Morning has
come.

Light

Birds tweeting and whistling tunes,
the sun is coming up from
behind the big tree.
Light shines upon the bench
The blossom falls down
Upon the grass.

Kerry Skinner (10)
Frinton-On-Sea Primary School

CRASH!

Crash! Bang! Wallop! It's raining cats and dogs.
Bash! Clatter! Clang! Pans hit the ground.
Ting! Smash! Boom! The rocket hits the moon.
Crack! Thump! Bump! Balls bounce around.
Why is everything so loud?

Waft, float, glide; the feather lands on the pillow.
Softly, slowly, carefully; the butterfly glides in the air.
Gently, calmly, smoothly; the balloon flies high.
Ahh, that's better!

Edward Evans (11)
Frinton-On-Sea Primary School

SADIE SAID

Sadie said to Sophie,
And Sophie said to Shane,
So Shane said to Sarah,
'We can win this game.'

Running around like maniacs,
Trying to get the ball,
Then all their chances ended,
When Sadie had a fall.

She slid across the polished floor,
And bumped into the benches.
Arms and legs flew up and out,
The teacher lost her dentures.

The teacher fell on Sarah,
Sarah gave a shout,
The headteacher then came running in,
She said, 'What's the fuss about?'

She got no further than the door,
Then she slid over too,
'That's enough,' she said to us,
'No more games for you.'

Cassie Thompson (11)
Frinton-On-Sea Primary School

DAWN IS COMING BY THE RIVER

The rays of golden sunlight break over the hills,
Dawn is coming by the river,
It glimmers on the grass and water,
Warmth revives the plants and animals,
Dawn is coming by the river,
Sparkling dew settles on leaves,
The bright light shines on a pebbly path,
Dawn is coming by the river,
A blaze of light reflects off the water's side
Dawn is coming by the river,
The grass blades reflect the sunlight like a
Curved mirror.
Dawn is coming by the river.

Sophie Gooch (11)
Frinton-On-Sea Primary School

A LIGHT HOUSE

In a light wood, there is a light house,
In that light house, there is a light room,
In that light room, there is a light cupboard,
In that light cupboard, there is a light shelf,
On that light shelf, there is a light box,
In that light box, there is a light bulb.

Thomas Brand (10)
Frinton-On-Sea Primary School

THE TWO GIRLS

There was a girl who had a curl
and one day she started to twirl her curl
and it began to whirl,
and swirl.

There was one day a girl who admired the girl with
the curl which she twirled,
She began to twirl her curl,
and you couldn't tell which girl began
to twirl her curl first,
and which girl admired the girl with the curl
that she twirled and started to twirl her curl.

Sadie Newell (10)
Frinton-On-Sea Primary School

DADS!

Dads always try their best, but never hard enough,
When they pick you up from school,
they embarrass you quite a lot,
They pick you up and swing you round
and kiss you on the cheek,
And call you lovey dovey words like
honey, darling and sweetpea.

Despite all this I love my dad,
And at the end of the day he's not that bad.

Leanne Gosford (11)
Frinton-On-Sea Primary School

DEATH ON THE TABLE

I stand, a knife in one hand
I take the handle by the end
There it is all alone
No one there so I don't have to share.

It sits on a cloth
I think
How should I do it
Quick or slow?

I put my hand in the air
I open my eyes
Nice and wide
I bring the knife down

Slit right through the middle
There, sits on the table
On the cloth
Two pieces of apple.

Matthew Lindsay (11)
Frinton-On-Sea Primary School

MY OLD BIKE

I love you though your seat is mouldy,
I love you though your frame is rusty,
I love you though your brakes are busted,
I love you though your tyres are flat,
I love you though your handlebars are bent,
I love you though your spokes are wonky,
I love you though you're as slow as a donkey.

Anthony Larvin (11)
Frinton-On-Sea Primary School

MYSTERIOUS NIGHT

Dark and depressing is the mysterious night
The way the moon looks in its creepy white eyes
A scary scarecrow you suddenly meet
Walking down the lonely dark street
You run across to the next tree
To hide away from the man you see
You think he's coming up towards you
To kidnap or stab someone right behind you
You suddenly realise you've been seen
Then you hear a blood-curdling scream.

Sarah Hall (10)
Frinton-On-Sea Primary School

I DON'T WANT TO BE A PILOT

I don't want to be a pilot
I don't want to be shot down
I don't want to be a pilot,
I don't want to end up on the ground
Dog fights
Loud guns
Planes soaring out of sight
Facing death every day
Grown men brawling
Engines stalling
Then exploding in mid flight.

Andrew Webster (11)
Frinton-On-Sea Primary School

MILLENNIUM BUG

'What's this Millennium Bug?' I hear
Every day throughout the year
Is it hairy, is it big?
Does it wear a curly wig?
Where does it live? Nobody knows
I hope it's not in my clothes
Will it bite you in the dark?
You'll soon find out, there'll be a mark
Has it got fangs and glowing eyes?
Nobody knows, everyone sighs
If you see it, close your lids
Cos it only tells lies to all us kids.

Abigail Alger (8)
Harlowbury CP School

MILLENNIUM

Millennium can come only once in a lifetime
I hope that the year 2000 comes in just fine.
I hope the computers don't all crash
And that the gas and electricity don't go out in a flash
Some will celebrate it in the Dome
I just wish everyone had a home
Some will dance all through the night
Fireworks will shine so bright
At 12 o'clock everyone will shout and cheer
To welcome in the new millennium year.

Emma Steven (11)
Harlowbury CP School

NANNY LILY

I love her beautiful soft skin,
She really keeps me warm.
When I'm with her I feel like I'm the luckiest girl in the world.
And when she gets up I shiver in the cold.
Her hair is as white as glittering crystals
And her cheeks are like roses in the sunlight.
When her clothes have just been washed,
They smell like spring just approaching
But when she has gone I will be in a world,
Of my own sadness.

Kylie Anne Doe (10)
Harlowbury CP School

THE MONSTER'S DEAD

Joy to the world, the monster's dead.

We kept its eyes and put them in pies,
We kept its nose and gave it to Rose.

Joy to the world, the monster's dead.

We kept its legs and turned them to pegs,
We kept its hands and mixed them with sand.

Joy to the world, the monster's dead.

We kept its bones and broke them with stones,
We kept its heart and pulled it apart.

Joy to the world, the monster's dead!

Martin Goodchild (10)
Milwards CP School

DAD

My dad is . . .

A tooth puller,
A money spender,
A good driver,
A food burner,
A long sleeper,
A brilliant footballer,
A big hugger,
A good mate,
A funny dad,
A slow runner,
A hard worker,
An excellent joker,
A beer drinker,
A rubbish drawer,
A fantastic father,
A chocolate lover,
A splendid person.

Lee Hattersley (10)
Milwards CP School

CAT

A fast eater,
A wall climber,
A chair clawer,
A fast drinker,
A fast runner,
A heavy sleeper.

Mark Franklin (10)
Milwards CP School

SQUIRREL CHASE

The squirrel's bushy tail sweeps
along the wide, bumpy tree,
darting swiftly to find his
supper of acorns.

He jumps down from the acorn tree,
he hides among the swaying green
long grass.

He digs his teeth into an acorn.
His sparkly ginger fur moults
as his fur becomes moist in
the dewy grass.
His shadow increases as
the sun moves round in the sky.

Melanie Dahm (10)
Milwards CP School

MY MUM

A big hugger,
A lovely person,
A hard worker,
A slow runner,
A good food burner,
An excellent first-aider,
A brilliant chatter,
A light sleeper,
A blood donor,
A chocolate eater.

Jonathan Stewart (9)
Milwards CP School

THE SEA

It moves with a slow ripple like a belly-dancer,
and at times thrashes like a black bull, with glowing red eyes.
It can be warm like tropical rain and
it can be cold, like a misty ice cube.
It can be hungry like a lion tearing limb from limb out of the waves.
It can be joyful when accompanied by playful children.
It can lonely like a puppy away from its mum.
It can be playful, crashing against the rocks
like a kitten with a ball of string.
It can be clever like an A-level student.
It can be shy like a child at a new school.

Lauren Roberts (11) & Ellie Bromage (10)
Milwards CP School

PINK POEM

Pink perfume smells perfect.
It smells like sweet, pink roses.
Pink is the blossom tree with small flowers blooming,
the kind you like to see when you've got a pink Loveheart.
Pink is the colour of the bridesmaid's dress you wear
when your best friend gets married.
Pink is the colour of a friendship put back together again.
Pink is the colour of a good relationship.

Gemma Watson (9)
Milwards CP School

THE MURKY OCEAN

Beneath the murky ocean,
there's a dogfish chasing a catfish
through the slimy seaweed.
Disgusting and horrible.
A dead shark on the surface,
a swordfish stabbing it to hell.
I look around, it's only a dream.
I go back on my sea journey.
A starfish smiles
as it glides along in the sea.
The freezing cold water
feels like little ice cubes
running along my back
as I swim, shivering.

Danny Milson (11)
Milwards CP School

BLUE

Blue is a bright, blue sky.
Blue is a baked blueberry pie.
Blue is the colour of dark bluebells.
Blue is the colour of the salty sea.
Blue is the colour of a cute blue tit.
Blue is the colour of the jumper on me.

Hayley Newman (10)
Milwards CP School

Lost Love

Beyond the blue mountains,
far beneath the sea, lies a
precious locket, lost many years ago.
Moving slowly across
silent sands
as the ships drift past,
moving the love backwards and forwards,
waiting to be picked up.
It floats along the dark waving
seaweed and rocks.
The sun shining
on the lost locket,
reflecting a reflection
through the icy, glassy waters.

Paul Taylor (10)
Milwards CP School

Blue

Blue is the bright blue sky.
Blue is the deep, dark sea.
Blue is the colour of my friend's bright eyes that gleam.
Blue is the colour of my favourite football team.

Charlotte Fargeot (9)
Milwards CP School

THE CALM, PEACEFUL, CORAL WAY

Deep down below the surface of
the colourful coral reef,
down near the bottom, deep, deep underneath,
opposite a sea shell, sparkling in the sun
an octopus is resting, his life is nearly done.
An old, crumbling turtle, making his way to die,
even in his sadness he has a twinkle in his eye.
This silence won't be disturbed by night or day,
so forever calm and peaceful this secret coral will stay.

Anna Calderon (10)
Milwards CP School

THE SHIP

The ship was flowing, then it was glowing,
It was like a small wave.
It was like a big cave.
The ship was very high,
It was nearly as tall as the sky.
The ship galloped across the sea,
While the captain was drinking a cup of tea.
It made a small wave, it was like a big cave.
The ship was coming last, and then it was coming fast.

Lee Tanner
Milwards CP School

THE WONDROUS LAKE

Between the lake's banks,
And the school of golden fish,
The lake wavers.
The sun reflects on the glittering lake.
Through the bridge there hangs strings of pink blossom.
Above the bridge, perched on it,
Are the doves cooing to the dusk.
Behind the doves, the sun sets, a violent pink.
Beneath the water level, the night seeks
Thousands of stickleback fish,
And below the bridge, there swims
An elegant, white swan.

Sarah Packer (11)
Milwards CP School

WHALE

Underneath the icy sea,
beyond the weeds,
lies a helpless killer whale
who's lost his family.
Wandering through the
manky shipwreck,
dark and dingy.
As it tumbles to the floor
it wails away.

Elliott Foster (11)
Milwards CP School

THE SEA MONSTER

Has a nose like a shiny bottle,
Has fins like sharp knives
Waiting to cut something,
Has black slithering strips
Running down his back,
Has swimming skills like snakes,
Slithering in the sea swiftly.

Natasha Freeman (10)
Milwards CP School

BULLIES

If people were flowers,
Bullies would be rough stinging nettles,
Under the bushes with dark, crispy colours.
They hide and wait to attack,
As the hand reaches for the ball.
The nettles stroke, gentle, soft and furry.
Suddenly, pain strikes the hand.
The bully has succeeded.

Amar Raja (10)
Milwards CP School

TORNADO

The trees were thrown up high,
Stabbing the sky,
Chewing up the land.
The tornado roared,
Down the trees poured,
Crashing loudly, like a brass band.

Amy Downes (11)
Milwards CP School

THE OCEAN

Underneath the ocean,
Underneath the clear ocean
That sparkles with pride,
Hovers a black shark
That has been sliced by a lethal weapon,
Which is a dreadful net.
The black shark, desperate for help
From the world above.
He's feeling angry,
Struggling for freedom.
And now it's time to go.

Luke Breeds (11)
Milwards CP School

FOUR WAYS OF LOOKING AT FISHING

You unleash the reel,
setting further into the distant water,
like a dart gliding through the air, never ending.
Your maggot wobbles and wriggles
before it hits the cold water.
You get a bite, you jump with joy,
like a man finding a golden ring.
The fish crawl and cry,
trying to get free.

Jamie Bowie (10)
Milwards CP School

THE SHINY STONE

Underneath the cloudy green river
behind the rocks and weed.
At ground level lies a smooth shiny stone
waiting to be selected.
To be dragged over the river bed,
and out into the salty sea.

Sam Lacey (10)
Milwards CP School

I WISH I HAD A CAT IN THE YEAR 2000

I wish I had a cat called Black
I don't mind if I have a dog,
or a flying bat, but I love cats.
I can take him to the Millennium Dome,
We could stay up late
and take him home.
Or we could take him to a dance,
And watch him prance,
And then I would have a little dance
And have some fun.
We could count Big Ben's bongs to 12.
Say 'Goodbye 1999,
Hello year 2000!'

Elleni Kyreikides (8)
Oaklands School

I Wonder What It's Going To Be Like In The Millennium!

I wonder what will happen in Italy and in Rome,
In Spain and in Sweden
And in the Millennium Dome.
Will there be fireworks?
Will there be lights?
Will there be colours?
Will the world improve?
Or get even worse!
Will there be peace?
Or will there be war?
Will there be fireworks?
Will there be lights?
And will the world party through the night!

Rebecca Bowen (8)
Oaklands School

Millennium

The year 2000 will be a millennium
Robbie Williams will be singing 'Millennium'
Go to Big Ben or stay in
Eat popcorn all night

Put the decorations up
Put the best at the top
Get ready to bop
Everyone says *party!*
Everyone's happy
They're already wacky
If you get tired say *goodnight!*

Brooke Painter (8)
Oaklands School

CELEBRATIONS 2000

C elebrating
E xciting
L ate nights
E lection
B anger fireworks
R ockets
A nimation
T ongue biting
I nviting people to parties
O utside parties
N erve racing

T eeth shattering
W hining
O h yes! Oh yes! Let's have a party

T eeth binding
H appiness
O k let's start
U nknown people
S pace
A nxious to have some champagne
N aughty children
D ome.

Emma Reeves (9)
Oaklands School

THE MILLENNIUM DOME

To think one thousand years ago
There might have been another Dome.
Another thousand years has passed,
Another thousand years at last.
The millennium is here.

We can stay up late and celebrate,
Not sleep a wink.
Just play and dance - and think
The millennium is here.

Stay up till four in the morning,
Stay till the day is dawning.
Up having loads of fun
Dancing with your dad and mum.
The millennium is here.

At last you go upstairs to bed
Feeling tired and nodding your head.
The year two thousand at last is here
Now wait another thousand years.
The millennium is here.

Maria Green (8)
Oaklands School

MY CAT AND MOUSE

I had a little cat
Who was rather fat.
I had a little mouse
Who was scared of the house.

My cat played with string
And my mouse had a great big ring.

I jumped on the stool
And dived in the pool
Because it was time for my bath.

I got out of the bath and continued
to play with my cat and mouse,
then it was time for bed.

Kirsty Louise Wright (11)
Oaklands School

CELEBRATION 2000

Celebration 2000
Got to go there.
Look around, have some fun.
Enjoy yourself in the big, bright sun.
Yeah! It's the millennium.
Save up your money,
Don't think it's not worth it.
Yeah! It's the millennium.
I'm going to go there.
Look at the fireworks.
Bang! Swish!
Over a big fat dish.
Yeah! It's the millennium.
If you go there,
You'll hear all the girls go
Robbie! Robbie!
Because it's the millennium.
I want to see Robbie sing.
Millennium . . . Yeah!

Louise Fowler (9)
Oaklands School

WHAT'S GOING TO BE HAPPENING IN THE YEAR 2000?

The celebration begins
In the Millennium Dome.
The fireworks go bang
The balloons go pop.

People party all night long
You stay up late and celebrate.

You go for trips by
The Dome, all alone.
You want to know
What's in the Dome?

People have been
Working hard
To get the Dome right.
It's going to be a
Fabulous night.
The year 2000
Has come.

Sophie Rose (9)
Oaklands School

CELEBRATION 2000

We celebrate the year 2000
With sparklers and fireworks
Parties and games
Staying up till midnight
And joining in the fun
Not long to wait . . .
For the New Year will have just begun.

Charlotte Crayfourd (8)
Oaklands School

THE MEAN RAT

There is a little mouse
        living inside my house.
And my poor little cat
        is scared of this mean rat.

But I am not scared of this mean rat,
        I can handle things like that.
I had to buy my cat a stool,
        because he's such a big fool.

Actually, I am scared of this mean rat,
        just like my stupid cat.
I need the stool, I am a fool.

        Help me Mummy now!

Clare Helen Leckie (10)
Oaklands School

THE SLY OLD RAT

There is a mouse
That lives in a house
He is a furry rat
Who lives in a hat.

The rat is scary
And he is hairy
I am scared of that rat
That lives in the hat.

There I am on a stool
Watching that sly old rat drool
Until I see my mum come in
I see that rat run into it din.

Ipek Hulya L'Aimable (10)
Oaklands School

THE CAT, THE RAT AND THE MOUSE

I have a little friend
On whom I can depend.
But there's a mean old rat
Who keeps scaring off my cat.

Once in my house
There was another mouse.
Who was kind to me
And all my family.

He wasn't like the rat
That had scared off my cat.
So in the end
The mouse was my friend.

And my good little cat
Was not scared of the rat
That lived in my grandad's old hat.

Sophie Jane Atalar (10)
Oaklands School

TEDDY BEARS

Teddy Bears are soft and fluffy
Some are neat and some are scruffy.
Some are pink and some are white,
Some are brown and some are bright.
Benjy, Boo Boo, Fluffy, Floppy,
All these names are rather soppy.
But if you've got a favourite bear
It's only important that you care.

Charlotte Bossick (9)
Oaklands School

THE WHITE TWITCHY MOUSE

As I stood on my tippy toes in my small old house
I saw on the floor a white twitchy mouse.
He stared back at me with his big, beady eyes
I tried to get my cat away with many, many tries.

As I wobbled on the stool holding my dear cat
I heard at the door a rat-a-tat-tat.
The mouse twitched his nose and scampered away
And there was I left with my dear ginger stray.

I looked everywhere for the white twitchy mouse
I looked in all the holes of my small old house.
I thought to myself 'Oh, where have you gone!'
And then I saw the mouse as he scampered along.

I was very pleased that the mouse and I met
And I decided to have it as my own special pet.

Rachel Taylor (11)
Oaklands School

THE MILLENNIUM BUG

The Millennium Bug is just like a slug.
It crawls all over the floor.
It flies up high into the sky
Also falls to the floor.
It goes into computers big or small
Then starts to ruin them all.

Jasmeet Kaur Chadha (9)
Oaklands School

MILLENNIUM DAYS

Trips on boats past the Dome
On and on the boat goes
Hear the fireworks go crackle then bang
You must see it, it's ever so much fun.

Millennium days are the best.
The government help the poor.
The homeless now have homes
And suffering is no more.

Millennium days are the best.
Everyone's happy - they're almost wacky.
Things have changed since last year
I hope millennium days will never end.

Jasmin Aujla (8)
Oaklands School

CELEBRATING 2000

I'd like to have a party in our street
I'd make beautiful invitations, oh so neat.
Inviting lots of famous people I'd like to meet.
Musical instruments playing classical music
while we eat.

I'd ask all my guests to come in fancy dress
To have a good time, but not to make a mess.
This party would last for hours, we'd all have
terrific fun.
We'd dance and eat and chat a lot
and go home with the rising sun.

Georgina Vincent (7)
Oaklands School

CELEBRATION 2000

C elebrations
E xciting
L uxurious
E njoy
B eing famous
R obbie Williams
A ctions
T ongue twisting
I nvitations
O utside parties
N ature courses

T he fun
W hining
O h joy

T eeth binding
H appiness
O n the road
U niverse
S pace
A nimation
N oisy
D evasted.

Gulgun Chakartash (8)
Oaklands School

MILLENNIUM DOME

There is the Millennium Dome
it looks like a big comb.
No! Forget that.
It looks like a big bowl.
Yes! That's right.

What's inside, I wonder what!
Let's look - just a peep.
Look! Some stairs
You wait here
I'll go upstairs.
No! Wait!
I'm actually rather scared.

'Five pounds fifty, please.'
'OK' I said and shook my head.
Only two pounds?
Oh no! Time to go home.

Sophie Wise (8)
Oaklands School

IN THE YEAR 2000

In the year 2000
I'll have a big party
I'll call all my friends
And dress up all tarty.

In the year 2000
In the dark air
With the moon shining bright
And the stars that glare.

In the year 2000
We will stay up late
I'll have a great time
Because we're all mates.

Lauren Jenkin (9)
Oaklands School

THE RACE

We line up in our shorts and tops
The race is about to begin.
We wait for the whistle to be blown
and then the race begins.

We try to get up at the front
but people just push us back.
It really is very hard
but we still head straight for the front.

In the middle of the race
there's a great big stream.
I nearly fell in, but luckily
I grabbed the mud, climbed the bank and
carried on with the track.

At the end of the race
I always feel proud.
Whenever I reach the end of a course
my mum always shouts 'Yeah!'

Annabel Petrou (9)
Oaklands School

CELEBRATION 2000

Children here, children there
Children having fun at the fair.
You know why?
Why?
Because it's the 2000th year.

Toffee apples, ice-cream and cakes,
Celebrations, parties and your mates.
Whizz go the fireworks
Lighting up your face.

Bing bang, bing bong
Celebrating all night long.
Take a breath, wait a minute,
What's all this about?

We wouldn't have the millennium
If Jesus hadn't have been born at the inn.

Victoria Edwards (8)
Oaklands School

MISSING MOG

Last night Mog and I got an awful scare
When we saw a mouse upon the stair.
It said to us 'Don't be afraid,
All I want is some marmalade!'

I jumped onto a nearby stool
The mouse replied 'You're such a fool!'
Mog wriggled and struggled to get free
At that moment, I scratched my knee!

Mog jumped free!
The stool tipped over, oh calamity!
Mousie found her marmalade
And tiptoed out into the glade.

I will never forget that emotional day
When mousie scared my Mog away.
I really miss him very much
So if you see him get in touch!

Camilla Atkins (11)
Oaklands School

CAT, MOUSE AND ME

Me and my cat had a peaceful time
Because we always spoke in mime
But when the mice all came in
There was such a terrible din.

I loved my kitten
We never got bitten
We had a safe house
Then came a white mouse
He came into my hut
And gave us both a bad cut.

Finally my cat plucked up the courage
And made the white mouse sniff and forage
He pounced on the rat
And that was the end of that.

Rachel Liane Diamond (11)
Oaklands School

CELEBRATION 2000

Excitement in the street
Friends and family rushing to meet.
Lots of parties with food and drink,
A special night out . . . what a treat!

Fireworks whizz
Champagne corks pop.
Disco music rocks
And the party never stops.

The year 2000 is very near
We all hold hands, shout and cheer.
When the clock strikes midnight
The balloons come down
And we know that the millennium is here.

Rebecca Bossick (8)
Oaklands School

ANIMAL

With a sharp red beak
And long clawed feet
These things are a sight
That you have to meet
They live in one country only
With the initials NZ
They have feathers - unlike you or me.

Sarah Frances Burnton (11)
Oaklands School

ANDY'S PETS

In Andy's room he keeps . . .
Ten green crocodiles
nine red baboons
eight big grey elephants.
Seven long slithery snakes
hanging from the light
six hungry lions hiding
under the bed.
Five blue whales
hiding in a fish tank
four brown dung beetles
living inside his bed.
Three spiders hanging on
his door knob
two earwigs climbing
up the wall.
And one guess what!

Daniel Howell (9)
Pear Tree Mead Primary School

MY CAT TWINKLE

Twinkle my love
We like her better than anyone else.
In her heart she has love.
Nice little twinkle, we love her to bits.
Kiss her and hug her.
Lovely and beautiful as she always is.
Eats and sleeps all day long
We love them all.

Sarah McCoy (9)
Pear Tree Mead Primary School

DINOSAURS

Some dinosaurs are big
Some dinosaurs are small
I don't care because I love them all.

My favourite is Raptor
He runs really fast,
He was great in the past.

All that is left is bones and teeth
And hear my pet -
T-rex roar!

David Jameson (10)
Pear Tree Mead Primary School

SPRING

S pring is cool, spring is warm
P addle in the paddling pool - it's cool
R ain, rain all day long non-stop rain
I n spring, flowers grow and trees grow buds and blossoms
N on-stop rain all day long
G o on, go on, go.

Outside - see everything grow and change.

Chloe Dyer (9)
Pear Tree Mead Primary School

PARROT

My parrot bites
He really can give you a fright.
He sits on your arm
Sometimes he's calm.
I might bring him to school
When it's nice and cool
He can sit on the table
Well, if he's able!
He likes books
He can give you funny looks
He likes the garden
Or did he say Kindergarten?
He likes me
He might have some tea.
He cost a thousand pounds
Sometimes he doesn't make a single sound
You don't know
He might do a to and fro!
By the time he's ninety-nine
You never know
He might chime!

Michelle Lillie (9)
Pear Tree Mead Primary School

AUTUMN

A nip in the air as you exit the house
Trees fit to burst with fruit
Fairy forests and golden leaves
Start to fall around me
Brittle leaves make a blanket on the floor
And skeleton trees claw the sky.

Christopher Dunning (11)
Rolph CE Primary School

AUTUMN

Sparkling webs
crispy, crunchy leaves
floating off the trees

Crunch crackle
the brittle leaves
crumple and cling together

The clouds whisper
letting a chilly breeze flow
they let out trickling rain

Skeleton trees appear
only a few fragile leaves remain.
Golden orange and yellow leaves
spread across the frosty roads.

Robyn Sawyer (11)
Rolph CE Primary School

AUTUMN

Crunchy fragile leaves,
a spine chilling crackle of fire
as I step on them,
when walking through dark
creepy woods of autumn
skeleton trees staring . . .
examining me.

Natasha Stibbard (11)
Rolph CE Primary School

AUTUMN

It's like snow as the leaves fall
There's embers of red, yellow and orange
Some still hang low in the wind
yet others are on the ground very still.
Until the wind blows and they go everywhere
like a tornado.

As autumn goes by it starts to get colder,
the webs got a sparkle to them
some people are playing conkers
yet others play with the leaves
but still there are the people snuggled warm in bed.

The hot dinners are coming now
and the warm apple pies.
Now the trees are going bald
almost like skeleton's I suppose
and the animals start hibernating
until the spring.

Linda Clark (11)
Rolph CE Primary School

AUTUMN

Sparrow leaves fighting in the air
twisting, curling.
Skeletal remains of once proud oaks
and ashes, stripped bare
Old man willow catches unsuspecting hair
with his vast twiggy claws.

William Smith (10)
Rolph CE Primary School

AUTUMN

Whispering willow winds
Skeleton claws crackling crisply
Scantily clad scattered tree trunks
Glistening gleaming reflections
on sparkling cobwebs
Golden shining leaves laying in
beds and beds
Covering the fragile soil that
lays beneath them.

Sarah Wallace (11)
Rolph CE Primary School

NOVEMBER

November, November
Cold, windy and rainy
November, November
Loud, noisy with fireworks
November, November
Smells from bonfires and old leaves
November, November
The cook cooking blackberry and apple crumble
November, November
The drink-seller selling blackberry whisky
November, November
Colourful leaves and bare trees
November, November
Sadness of war and poppies
November, November!

James Nott (11)
St Anne's Preparatory School, Chelmsford

A HOSTAGE? ME? WHY ME?

A hostage? Me? Why me?
I was only doing my job
But what punishment is this
being trapped in a smelly old cell?
With a blindfold across my eyes.
No one else to talk to
living in permanent darkness.

A hostage? Me? Why me?
I was only in the wrong place
at the wrong time.
I was only looking around for a good place to write about
when they grabbed me, pulled me back.
Tore my jacket, hit me on the back with a rifle,
Yanked my hair and chained my hands.

A hostage? Me? Why me?
I was only doing it for my newspaper
I was asked questions
But I didn't answer
I was hit again and answered.
'Are you English?
Do you work for the Government?
Where is your base? Do you work for MI5?

A hostage? Me? Why me?
I was only helping out.
I worked for a charity
to bring help to hungry people
and clear away dangerous landmines
with Princess Diana.
This satisfied my captors,
And I was taken back to a town
and released.

Meghann Reeder (10)
St Anne's Preparatory School, Chelmsford

NOISES IN NOVEMBER

Bang! Bang! Go the fireworks.
Woo! Go some
Red, blue, green, yellow, purple
Beautiful in the sky.

Wow! Go people when they slip on ice.
Crunch! When people stamp on the leaves
Red, yellow, brown
That cover the ground.

Bang! Goes the cannon to be quiet
for two minutes to remember the
men who fought in the war.
Sh! Sh! Sh!
Fields of red poppies.

Joanna Eagar (11)
St Anne's Preparatory School, Chelmsford

THE LAST DAY OF TERM

Today's the day
When we do nothing but play
Dance and daydream
You can do it all the way

Kiss each other goodbye
And give a little sigh
Don't be too sad
You should be glad

You can go really mad
Although it seems bad
You may fly high above
Like a peaceful dove

When it all ends
You go round the bend
Start a new life
With a new friend

Rebecca Eleady-Cole (10)
St Anne's Preparatory School, Chelmsford

MY DAD

I often think that my dad
(and he admits it too)!
I often think that he is mad!
If you met him, you'd think that too!

He always knows that there is
No fun in being good.
And I know I'd miss the *old* him
If he started being good.

I really, really love him.
I'm glad he'll never change.
He's a hero in his own way,
And everyone . . . remember this.

He's my dad and my dad only!

Diana Bebby (10)
St Anne's Preparatory School, Chelmsford

HOSTAGE

I was put in a room
with a blindfold on.
Starving hungry all day long.
Get to go to the toilet three times a day.
All I could hear was
a guard . . .
With nothing to say.

A few years on
another man came.
We sat: no talking, no food, no games
The next day came
We peeped out of our blindfolds
And felt a lot better.

The day arrived
I was set free.
It's a very happy ending.
Until I was seen
My dad was sad
And told me that day
that my mother had died.

Now I am free
I live a happy life.
Until the moments when memories
flood back in time.

Nicola De Rienzo (11)
St Anne's Preparatory School, Chelmsford

ME, As A Hostage

'Hello! Have you come to visit me?
I honestly hope you have.'
The guards plod up and down the corridor
So fierce are they
I do wish I could see
how my girlfriend's getting on.
She's miles across the open sea.
I'm sick of food being flung at me
I want to travel home
Across the timeless sea.

The sea I vaguely remember
'Where do I see it?' You say.
I see it in my mind
where everything's clear.
Sometimes I wonder why I signed up
for this job
Now I know
It's because I wished to be free
Not free from captivity
But free from war
And other things.
Soon I shall be ever free
When I pack my bags for Heaven.

James Deering (11)
St Anne's Preparatory School, Chelmsford

HOSTAGE

It's cold, damp and dreadful
I am scared stiff
Sitting in my chair
Waiting, listening.

Who? What? Where? Why?
Why me?
What did I do?
Where am I?
Who did this dreadful deed?

I miss my family
I can picture them now.
Sitting at the table
Wondering where I am.

I hope someone will save me
From this dreadful place.
The food is poisoned
It smells so bad
I'm really homesick now.

It's cold, damp and dreadful
I am scared still
Sitting in my chair
Waiting, listening.

Emma Charman (10)
St Anne's Preparatory School, Chelmsford

MAYBE

Maybe I'll get through the day
Maybe I'll see the angels
But who's to know what's yet to come?
Misery, pain and terror
Suffocate me
Wrapping round me
There's no escape.

Maybe I'll see the bright sun again
Maybe I'll be in darkness forever
Never knowing what's going on around me
I have forgotten
Forgotten what love is
But I know I'll never forget the terror
And the silence around me.

This poem is about John McCarthy - the hostage.

Emily Low (10)
St Anne's Preparatory School, Chelmsford

MY HOUSE

I   is for impatient for the shower
N   is for nagging in the kitchen

T   is for tarantulas we see in the bath ahhg!
H   is for hearing 'Where are my shoes?'
E   is for eating breakfast on the run

M   is for Mum moaning
O   is for omelette landing on the floor
R   is for running out the door
N   is for nothing packed in my bag
I   is for 'I'm going to be late!'
N   is for nervous for the test today
G   is for goodbye and have a nice day.

Amy Simons (11)
St Mary's CE School, Hatfield Broad Oak

BEING A DRAGON

Being a dragon is not all it's cracked up to be
Blowing fire every night
It costs you ringing the fire brigade
Think of the phone bill.
Claws crack and food gets stuck in under.
So if you're thinking of being a dragon
I would change your mind.
A cat or dog would be a better choice.
Breath awful
Take a mint, they said to me,
no hope of me finding a mate or a date.
It takes till midnight to clean my teeth
and remember the points.

Maximilian Adolphe (9)
St Mary's CE School, Hatfield Broad Oak

DRAGONS CREEP

Dragons creep like mice
Round and up they fly
And silver tails and golden wings shimmer in the sky.
Grim faces tremble and some scream with fear.
'Oh dragons' they cry 'don't come here!'
'No!' thinks dragon 'there's food down there.'

Creep and slither through the grass
Look at me fly.
You can't hear me 'cos you'll soon die.

Creep and slither through the grass
Across the driveway down the path.
In the house and up the stairs,
Open wide - *snap, you're dead!*

Isabelle Pemberton (11)
St Mary's CE School, Hatfield Broad Oak

SWINGS

Swings, swinging, high in the big blue sky
I thought I'd never go so high in the big blue sky
It was then I thought I could fly
In the big blue sky.

Louise Routledge (9)
Westerings School